EDITOR: LEE JOHN

 MEN-AT-A

LOUIS XV's ARMY (1) CAVALRY & DRAGOONS

Text by
RENÉ CHARTRAND
Colour plates by
EUGÈNE LELIÈPVRE

First published in Great Britain in 1996 by Osprey, an imprint of Reed Consumer Books Ltd., Michelin House, 81 Fulham Road, London SW3 6RB
and Auckland, Melbourne, Singapore and Toronto

© Copyright 1996 Reed International Books Ltd.

All rights reserved. Apart from any fair dealing for the purpose of private study, research, criticism or review, as permitted under the Copyright, Designs and Patents Act, 1988, no part of this publication may be reproduced, stored in a retrieval system, or transmitted in any form or by any means, electronic, electrical, chemical, mechanical, optical, photocopying, recording or otherwise, without the prior permission of the copyright owner. Enquiries should be addressed to the Publishers.

ISBN 1 85532 602 7

Filmset in Great Britain by KDI, Newton le Willows
Printed through World Print Ltd, Hong Kong

Publisher's note
Readers may wish to study this title in conjunction with the following Osprey publications:

MAA 285 *King George's Army 1740–93 (1)*
MAA 289 *King George's Army 1740–93 (2)*
MAA 292 *King George's Army 1740–93 (3)*
MAA 236 *Frederick the Great's Army (1) Cavalry*
MAA 240 *Frederick the Great's Army (2) Infantry*
MAA 248 *Frederick the Great's Army (3) Specialist*
MAA 271 *The Austrian Army 1740–80 (1) Cavalry*
MAA 276 *The Austrian Army 1740–80 (2) Infantry*
MAA 280 *The Austrian Army 1740–80 (3) Specialist*
MAA 203 *Louis XIV's Army*

If you would like to receive more information about Osprey Military books, The Osprey Messenger is a regular newsletter which contains articles, new title information and special offers. To join free of charge please write to:

**Osprey Military Messenger
PO Box 5, Rushden
Northants NN10 6YX**

Dedication: To Luce

Author's note
This book is the first in a series of five devoted to the organisation, uniforms and weapons of the largest military force in 18th-century western Europe: Louis XV's French army. This first volume will examine the cavalry of the royal guard, the heavy cavalry and dragoons of the line. Subsequent volumes will cover the infantry of the guard and the infantry of the line recruited in France, and the numerous foreign infantry regiments, the light troops (including hussars), the auxiliary corps such as the artillery and the engineers, and the numerous types of militia, some of which served as full-time conscript troops. The final volume will examine the colonial troops and militias in New France, the West Indies, Africa and India, as well as marines and other naval troops based in France. All will be illustrated by contemporary illustrations and portraits, and some 40 colour plates, each with several figures. When completed, it is hoped that the collection will form the most complete account of the organisation and uniforms of Louis XV's army published for a century.

In general, the hues of green and blue tended to be darker during Louis XV's reign; blue, for instance, was said to be an azure or royal blue shade in 1715, but Louis XV preferred a much darker blue as Gudenus shows in 1735. Grey-white cloth for uniforms was basically undyed natural wool which could vary from cream white to light grey.

Artist's note
Readers may care to note that the original paintings from which the colour plates in this book were prepared are available for private sale. All reproduction copyright whatsoever is retained by the Publisher. All enquiries should be addressed to:

M. Eugène Lelièpvre,
33 rue Boileau,
92120 Montrouge,
France

The Publishers regret that they can enter into no correspondence upon this matter.

LOUIS XV's ARMY (1) CAVALRY & DRAGOONS

INTRODUCTION

In 1715 the elderly 'Sun King' Louis XIV passed away and the throne of France devolved to his five-year-old great grandson, crowned in 1723 as Louis XV. The first 20 years of his reign were generally peaceful, a marked contrast to the war-like disposition of the previous king, and this was greatly appreciated by the people of France, who nicknamed their young king *Le bien aimé* – the beloved. After the rigid style of pomp and circumstance dear to Louis XIV, the new reign heralded a more relaxed and debonair atmosphere in society.

France had a population of between 22 and 25 million at that time, and maintained the largest standing army in Europe. In peacetime it might have amounted to about 200,000 men; in times of war, it could be anything up to half a million. The majority of the troops were stationed along France's borders with Flanders, Germany and Italy, with a few thousand garrisoning seaports and the colonies.

Yet France could hardly be termed a military society. It had approximately one regular soldier per 110 inhabitants in peacetime and one per 65 in wartime, compared to one in 27 in peace and one in 14 in war in a military state such as Prussia. The ratio of officers to men in France was very high: one in 11 enlisted men in the 1740s compared to Prussia's one in 29. Thus up to half of the army's budget for pay went to officers and, proportionally, the French army cost about a third more than that of Prussia.

A substantial part of Louis XV's army consisted of numerous regiments of guard cavalry, heavy cavalry and dragoon regiments, all of which were considered the best and noblest part of the army. These many units form the subject matter of this first volume.

THE ROYAL GUARD CAVALRY

The various guard cavalry units were meant to be the elite of the army, gathering some of the best and

King Louis XV, c.1730. This was the official portrait in the early part of the reign. Many copies were made by the studio of Van Loo, distributed in the provinces and the colonies to be hung in governors' palaces and fortresses. (Fortress Louisbourg National Historic Site)

bravest soldiers, to form a large and powerful reserve that could take the field and be an example for all to follow. The corps of the *Maison du Roi* (the king's household) were divided into two groups. First were the guard units *du dedans du Louvre* which served near the king, inside the royal palaces of the Louvre and Versailles. These included the Gardes du Corps. The second group of guard units, *du dehors du Louvre* (outside the palace), were the Gendarmes de la Garde, the Chevaux-légers de la Garde, the Mousquetaires de la Garde and the Grenadiers à Cheval. Since most of the

François Antoine d'Andlau, Scottish Company, Gardes du Corps, c.1742. Blue coat with red cuffs and lining, silver lace and buttons, St. Louis cross hanging from a scarlet ribbon, red waistcoat laced silver, black breast plate with blue velvet belts and lining laced silver, silver laced tricorn with white feather. (Private collection. Photo courtesy U.A. Koch)

cavalry of the guards *du dedans* had blue uniforms, they were nicknamed *la maison bleue* (the blue household). For the same reason, the cavalry of the guards *du dehors* was nicknamed *la maison rouge* (the red household).

In addition to these units was the Gendarmerie de France. On campaign, it was considered as a reserve division of the guard cavalry, since it stood on its own. Elitist, establishment and not part of the line cavalry, it had precedence (after the guard cavalry), since it answered directly to the king. Furthermore, the king, members of the royal family and princes were captains of its 16 companies.

While some units were of foreign origin, especially from Scotland, by the reign of Louis XV they were almost entirely recruited from the sons of the French nobility. The strength of these units was considerable: a cavalry company in the guard could be as large as a regiment in the line cavalry. The numbers of officers and men given below did vary from time to time, but only by ten or 20 men and a few officers. In wartime a cavalry company could have some 3,800 officers and men, including over 1,300 of the Gendarmerie. All members of the guard cavalry and the Gendarmerie had officer status in the line cavalry, captains were equivalent to colonels down to troopers being equivalent to sub-lieutenants.

Whatever their rank, members of the guard cavalry certainly regarded themselves as nobility and lived in style; for instance each Garde du Corps trooper had a servant. Naturally, the expense of these corps to the royal purse was enormous and, towards the end of Louis XV's reign reductions were increasingly made; ultimately this led to many corps being disbanded in the next reign.

The king himself approved the uniforms of each unit of the guard. Several soldiers would be paraded before the sovereign, each wearing a uniform featuring proposed alterations. Guard cavalry uniforms were meant to be splendid, and even private troopers had gold or silver lace on their coats. Blue lined red was the livery of Bourbon kings, and the uniforms of the royal guard units always had at least one of those colours.

The king's livery lace ornamented the uniforms of musicians in most units and it is important to explain this peculiar ornament. It came in two styles:

1) the basic livery lace, usually about an inch wide and sometimes called the 'small' livery, was a red or crimson lace with a white chain thereon;

2) the 'grand' livery was composed of a white central lace with red triangles which was edged on each side by the basic red or crimson lace with a white chain. This made it about two and a half to three inches wide. There was also a narrow livery edging lace of white with red lines.

In the guards, except for a few exceptions detailed below, the musicians' coats were almost covered with the king's 'grand' livery, often with silver lace replacing the central white and red lace. Their weapons, be they swords, pistols or muskets, while following general trends, were of models peculiar to each unit and had luxurious features such as elaborate gilded etchings.

Gardes du Corps

The Life Guards or Body Guards, consisted of four companies, each equivalent in strength to a small line cavalry regiment: 21 officers including a surgeon and a chaplain; some 400 NCOs and men (reduced in 1737 to 330), which were divided into two squadrons of three 'brigades' each. The senior company, dating back to 1440, was the 'Scottish company'. It had first been formed with Scots, but by the 16th century was recruiting Frenchmen. It had an additional 24 elite men known as *Gardes de la Manche* (literally 'Guards of the Sleeve'), meaning they stood so close to the king as to be brushed by his sleeves. The Gardes de la Manche formed a special squad of the king's most personal guards during ceremonies, and two of these guardsmen could always be found just behind the king, even during church services.

The three 'French' companies had been raised in 1475, 1479 and 1516, and were numbered the 1st, 2nd and 3rd French companies respectively. A Life Guard detachment was always near the king, wherever he went. They posted guards outside the rooms where he slept, escorted his food, sword in hand, from the kitchens to his table, and generally kept an eye on whoever came near. The Gardes du Corps only went on campaign if the king did. During his reign, Louis XV led his army in Flanders only during the War of Austrian Succession in 1744, 1745 and 1747. Thus, the last battle at which the Gardes du Corps were present was Lawfeld, fought on 1 July 1747.

They were armed with pistols, swords and flint-lock carbines. Rifled carbines were issued to nearly a quarter of the men in each company. The Scottish company's broadswords were Scottish claymores with steel basket guards, whereas the three other companies had the French-style heavy cavalry sword. A blackened breastplate was worn in battle. The Gardes du Corps wore bandoleers over the left shoulder to carry their musket and ammunition. Each company's bandoleers were garnished with silver lace to give them a checked appearance. Each company had bandoleers and housings of a distinctive colour: the Scottish company had white bandoleers and red housings, the 1st French company had green bandoleers and housings, the 2nd French company had blue bandoleers and housings and the 3rd French company had yellow bandoleers and housings. The housings were edged with a broad silver lace. There was no fixed colour for the horses of the NCOs and troopers, but blacks and dark bays were preferred.

The standard uniform for all companies was a blue coat with red cuffs and lining, silver buttons and silver lace at the buttonholes and edging the coat. The cuffs had two rows of lace; the pocket flaps had two rows with an additional lace framing the whole pocket flap. The back and sleeve seams were all decorated with a wide silver lace from about 1730.[1] The waistcoat was

Trooper of the Gendarmes of the Guard, c.1750. This company, dressed in scarlet with black velvet cuffs, used liberal amounts of gold lace on its uniforms and housings. (Anne S.K. Brown Military Collection, Brown University)

red with silver buttons and lace; breeches and stockings were red; cavalry boots were black; and hats were silver-laced. In the middle of the 18th century, the hat cockades are described as white and green for the Scottish company, and white with the colour of the bandoleer for the three French companies. However they are also shown as black or blue and white, and there seem to have been no fixed rules.

Officers wore the same uniform colours as the men, richly decorated with silver lace at the buttonholes, seams, edges, pocket flaps and cuffs. They had white plumes on the hats, and their housings had at least a double row of silver lace. All officers were to be mounted on grey horses.

From 1755, an undress surtout embroidered with silver was also worn by the Gardes du Corps. It was probably blue with red cuffs with buttonholes embroidered in silver.

There were six trumpeters and one kettledrummer per company. They wore blue velvet coats with false sleeves in the back and were almost covered with wide silver lace so that the blue showed in narrow strips

---

[1] How exactly this lace was set remains a mystery. Large loops with rounded ends are shown as early as 1735 by Gudenus and later in the 1760 manuscript. A painting by Parrocel c.1735 shows an officer with large rounded loops, as does a portrait of the 1740s. But loops with more pointed ends are also shown by Delaistre (1720-24) and by Chéraux, whose 1757 publication shows uniform styles that could be up to ten years earlier.

Guardsman of the Gardes de la Manche, the elite squad from the Scottish Company of the Gardes du Corps (Life Guards), c.1750, wearing the embroidered cassock over his uniform coat and armed with a richly etched partisan for service near the king. (Anne S.K. Brown Military Collection, Brown University)

between the silver. The red waistcoat had broader lace and the breeches were also red. The silver-laced hats had white plumes. Belts were covered with silver lace. Trumpets were of brass with silver cords and tassels, kettles of silver and banners blue with the royal arms richly embroidered and fringed in gold and silver. Housings were of the company colour, with a broad silver lace and a slightly narrower lace just above.

The 24 Gardes de la Manche of the Scottish company wore a luxurious cassock of white silk shaped like an 'antique' cuirass with skirts over the regular uniform coat. It was covered with magnificent embroidery in gold, silver and other colours that enhanced the work. It covered the entire garment – palms, laurels 'and all sorts of trophies'. The king's badge, the sun and the motto *NEC PLURIBUS IMPAR* were embroidered over the palms and laurel on the breast and at the back. The skirts and short sleeves were also profusely embroidered with trophies and floral designs.

The polearm was a gilded partisan head with elaborate engraving mounted on a pole covered with blue velvet and gold nails and a large silver tassel. For highly ceremonial state occasions, such as the coronation of Louis XV, in 1724, a squad of Gardes de la Manche wore, with the embroidered white cassock, an all-white silk 'antique' uniform consisting of a coat, baggy breeches, stockings, white shoes, white hat with white plumes. For state mourning they wore black.

Gendarmes de la Garde; Chevaux-légers de la Garde

A company of Gendarmes de la Garde (Men-at-Arms of the Guard), raised in 1611, and a company of Chevaux-légers de la Garde (Light Horse of the Guard), raised in 1593. Each company was mounted and consisted of 19 officers and 200 NCOs and men, including four trumpeters and one kettledrummer per company. Members in these units were expected to be of good birth and income. They were armed with pistols and swords, and in 1746 added muskets. Both companies had bay horses except for the officers of the Gendarmes, who were mounted on greys. They were quartered at Versailles and were disbanded in 1787. From 1744, the Chevaux-légers also served as cadre to a select military academy for 100 young noblemen who were considered part of the unit and wore its uniform.

Both the Gendarmes and the Chevaux-légers wore red coats lined with red and with black velvet cuffs. The lace at the buttonholes on the breast, cuffs and pockets was set pointed until the middle of the 18th century, when it was set in large rounded buttonholes. Gold lace edged the coat and the seams. The Gendarmes always had all-gold lace and gold buttons on the uniform and gold edging the red housings. The colours of the Chevaux-légers were more complicated: their red coats had, by the 1740s, black lining rather than red. They had broad gold lace on the uniform and housings, with silver thread set at the centre of the buttonholes and edging the gold lace on their red housings. The buttons of the Chevaux-légers were silver and the hat lace continued to be gold and silver mixed, until the 1750s, when the buttons became silver and gold mixed and the hat lace and housings were edged with gold only.

For both companies the waistcoat was of buff leather edged with company lace. By the 1740s the waistcoat was often of buff cloth, with buttonholes and edging of gold lace, with gold buttons for the Gendarmes and silver for the Chevaux-légers. Red breeches and stockings and black cavalry boots were worn. The Gendarmes' hat was edged with lace and garnished with white plumes and a black cockade. For the Chevaux-légers the cockade was white. From 1762 both companies added black velvet collars, lapels and turn-backs to the dress coat and adopted black velvet housings. Officers of both companies wore the same colours as the men, but their uniforms and housings were elaborately embroidered with lace.

In November 1743 the Chevaux-légers were also granted an undress uniform for campaigns and when travelling with the king. This consisted of a scarlet coat lined with red, small round cuffs and lapels of black velvet, buttonholes of narrow gold lace, silver buttons, a gold shoulder strap with silver fringes on the right shoulder, buff waistcoat with buttonholes of narrow gold lace and silver buttons, a gold-laced hat with white cockade and boots of soft leather.

Initially white-buff belts edged with lace were worn by both units, but by the 1740s the Chevaux-légers had changed to a black velvet waist-belt edged with gold with a silver central line.

Trumpeters and kettledrummers of the Gendarmes wore a special red livery with false sleeves and wings, lavishly ornamented with gold lace. Those of the Chevaux-légers wore the king's livery in blue velvet lined red with the edging lace of gold, then alternating silver and gold lace strips. The kettle and trumpet banners were blue with elaborate gold embroidery; both units had the royal arms at the centre.

Grenadiers à Cheval de la Garde

This company (Horse Grenadiers of the Guard), raised in December 1676, was recruited from the bravest grenadiers in the army. It had ten officers, 130 NCOs and troopers (including four drummers) and a chaplain, and could serve mounted or on foot. It was disbanded in 1776.

Their uniform, originally red, changed in 1692 to a blue coat with red cuffs, lining, waistcoats, breeches and stockings, and silver buttons and lace. The coat was edged with a narrow silver lace and, from around 1730, the coat was also garnished with wide pointed silver loops at the buttonholes. By 1745 the coat loops were worn in pairs and had the ends rounded instead of pointed. Officers and men wore a distinctive cap of red cloth turned up with fur. During Louis XV's reign the cap's red bag assumed a peculiar shape, pointing towards the rear with silver lace seams, while the fur in front was raised. The Horse Grenadiers had black leather dragoon gaiters which buckled at the side. They

Trooper of the Scottish Company and standard bearer of the First French Company of the Gardes du Corps, 1760. The company's six standards were yellow embroidered with silver. The standards of the other companies were also of the colour of the company bandoleers. (Royal Library, Madrid)

also had black cavalry boots, but rarely wore them. After 1762 red lapels with silver loops were added to the coat and a silver plate to the front of the grenadier cap.

The Horse Grenadiers were armed with pistols, carbines and curved sabres and had pouches for their grenades. They also had axes and other tools like dragoons. The enlisted men (but not the officers) were required to wear large black moustaches to make them look more fearsome and warlike. Housings were blue-laced with silver. The unit appears to have been mounted on bays.

Officers had the same uniforms as the men but with more lace on their coats. In 1720 they had silver lace on the coat's buttonholes and a wide lace edging each side of the buttonholes; their coat cuffs had elaborate silver lacing. By the 1730s the coat seams were also laced silver, as were the buttonholes with wide pointed loops, except the cuffs which had wide silver laces.

The Horse Grenadiers, being considered a dragoon-type corps, had drummers instead of trumpeters and wore the king's livery trimmed with silver lace. The drums were blue with the king's arms on the front.

Mousquetaire de la Garde

(Musketeers of the Guard.) There were two companies: the grey and the black musketeers, according to the colour of their horses. Each company had 17 officers, 200 NCOs and troopers (including six drummers and four hautbois) and ten staff, including a surgeon and three treasurers. Each company formed a squadron, which had four brigades. As the Musketeers were to serve both on foot and on horses, somewhat like dragoons, they had drummers instead of trumpeters, and infantry-style colours when serving on foot as well as cavalry guidons when serving mounted. Besides their guard services, the musketeer companies acted as a military academy for young noblemen, often from the higher nobility. Both companies were disbanded in 1775.

All-red coats were worn by both companies, laced with gold for the 1st company, silver for the 2nd. The distinctive lacing also edged the hats and buff bandoleers of both companies. The waistcoat, breeches and stockings were also red, and the waistcoat was laced with the company's lace. Hats' plumes were white.

The musketeers had black cavalry boots with spurs fixed in. For service on foot, they wore shoes. Housings were red, edged with gold or silver lace depending on the company. Their arms consisted of swords, pistols, and flintlock muskets. When serving on foot, the brigadiers had halberds.

The most distinctive feature of their uniform was the blue sleeveless coat (called a *soubreveste*). This garment would be slipped over the head, somewhat like a modern 'poncho', and fastened at the waist by a blue and silver belt. The soubreveste was lined with red and edged with two silver laces at each side. It had each company's distinctive white crosses edged with narrow silver lace on the breast and at the back; the tips of the crosses each had a gold lily. The 1st company had three gold and red flames at the angles of the cross; the 2nd company had five yellow and silver flames at the angles. The maréchal des logis wore a soubreveste with the royal cypher embroidered in gold on the skirt and edged with five silver laces; brigadiers had four silver laces, and sub-brigadiers had three.

Officers wore the all-red coat richly trimmed with company lace but not the soubreveste. In battle they wore richly engraved steel breast and back plates.

The Musketeers had drummers since they were considered a mounted infantry-type of corps. In practice the drummers were mounted. They wore the red coat,

Trooper of the company of Chevaux-légers (Light Horse) of the Guard, c.1750. The lace was gold but buttonholes were stitched with silver and housings also had silver as well as gold lace. (Anne S.K. Brown Military Collection, Brown University)

Standard bearers of the Gendarmes and the Chevaux-légers of the Guard, 1760. Each company had four standards of white silk embroidered in gold and silver and had central panels painted in natural colours. (Royal Library, Madrid)

waistcoat and breeches rather than the blue royal livery. Their soubreveste was the same colour as the men's, but also had false sleeves at the back and wings at the shoulders and was practically covered with broad silver lace. The crosses were put upon the silver lace on the chest and back of the soubreveste. Their skirts, unlike those of the officers and men, had elaborately laced pockets. The drums were smaller than those of the infantry, and were blue, with the king's arms painted on the front. The drum collars were blue edged with silver. The drummers had housings similar to those of the men of their respective companies, but they were mounted on white horses.

There were a number of noblemen serving with the Musketeers above the allowed establishment as *surnuméraires*. They had the same red uniform but did not wear the blue soubreveste, and they served dismounted.

Gendarmerie de France

(The Men at Arms of France.) The oldest company was the Scottish, dating back to 1422. It was the only Gendarmerie company until 1647, when the Gendarmes d'Orléans were raised. In 1660 the Gendarmes de la Reine and the Chevaux-légers de la Reine were raised for Queen Marie-Thérèse. Thereafter other Gendarmes and Chevaux-légers companies were raised until the last five of its 16 compa-

Companies of Gendarmerie

Company	Date raised	Bandoleer trim
Gendarmes Écossais	(1422)	Yellow
Gendarmes Anglais	(1667)	Violet
Gendarmes Bourguignon	(1668)	Green
Gendarmes de Flandre	(1673)	Orange
Gendarmes de la Reine	(1660)	Red
Chevaux-légers de la Reine	(1660)	Red
Gendarmes du Dauphin	(1666)	Blue
Chevaux-légers du Dauphin	(1663)	Blue
Gendarmes de Bretagne	(1690)	Yellow
Chevaux-légers de Bretagne	(1690)	Violet
Gendarmerie d'Anjou	(1669)	Green
Chevaux-légers d'Anjou	(1689)	Orange
Gendarmes de Berry	(1690)	Red
Chevaux-légers de Berry	(1690)	Red
Gendarmes d'Orléans	(1647)	Blue
Chevaux-légers d'Orléans	(1647)	Blue

Campaign uniform for the troopers (left) and officers (right) of the Chevaux-légers of the Guard, 1760. This dress was approved by the king in November 1743. (Royal Library, Madrid)

nies in 1690. Strength could vary from five officers, eight NCOs and 40 troopers (including two trumpeters and a kettledrummer) in peacetime to 75 troopers per company in wartime. Some companies were called Gendarmes while others would be Chevaux-légers but there was no real difference; all were actually heavy cavalry units.

The corps was in many battles, and its reckless charges by young bloods of the nobility made this division famous for its bravery. They were especially noted for their successful charges at Fontenoy and Lawfeld, during the War of Austrian Succession. The Seven Years War put a shadow on their renown, however. At Minden, which was to be their last engagement, they were badly mauled by the Anglo-Prussian forces, and their camp equipage was captured by the enemy. In 1763 the six Chevaux-légers companies were amalgamated into the Gendarmerie companies. There were further reductions in 1772, and the corps was finally disbanded in 1788. It never had anything to do with police work, but its name was adopted by police units during the French Revolution and has continued in countries all over the world.

At the beginning of Louis XV's reign all companies had the same uniform: an all-red coat with silver buttons and a silver lace around the cuffs. The silver lacing could vary according to the king's wishes. Around 1730, more silver lace was added, edging the pockets and the front of the coat. The waistcoat was buff with silver buttons, and a silver lace edging was added around 1730; this waistcoat silver lace was said to be mixed with black silk in the 1750s. The breeches and stockings were red, and black cavalry boots were worn. The hat was silver-laced with a black cockade.

Housings were red laced silver and embroidered with the cypher or badge of the captain of each company, for instance, the intertwined crowned 'L' for the king or the crowned dolphins for the dauphin, except in the company of Burgundy, which bore the ragged cross of that province.

Troopers were armed with pistols, a silver-hilted heavy cavalry sword and a rifled carbine. Up to 1730 the shoulder bandoleer to hook on the carbine was buff edged with silver for all companies. Thereafter different colours were adopted by individual companies.

As the table shows, some units of Gendarmes and of Chevaux-légers with the same designation had the same colours. To differentiate one from the other, the Chevaux-légers would have a lighter hue (since they were 'light' cavalry). Hence the Chevaux-légers du Dauphin actually had a light-blue bandoleer.

The trumpeters and kettledrummers of the Gendarmerie de France usually wore the king's livery of blue lined with red with silver lace added in between the livery lace. However, those of the companies of La Reine wore the queen's own livery, a red coat, lined and cuffed with blue and trimmed with a blue lace with a white chain, and silver lace as well. Those of Orléans also wore the duke's red-lined-blue livery with a lace of white with blue diamonds.

Officers had the same uniform as the men but their coats had more silver lace – at the buttonholes and at the seams of their coats. Officers (but not the men) wore a breast-plate over the waistcoat. They were armed with a pair of pistols and a silver hilted heavy cavalry sword.

Gardes du Corps de Monsieur[2] Gardes du Corps du Comte d'Artois

(Life Guard of Monsieur, Life Guard of the Count of Artois.) Near the end of his reign, Louis XV authorised a personal guard for each of his two grandsons, Monsieur le Comte de Provence (younger brother of Louis XVI, who became Louis XVIII in 1814) and the Comte d'Artois (later Charles X). The Gardes du Corps de Monsieur were raised in April 1771 of two companies of 50 men each, and wore a red coat with blue collar, cuffs and lining, red waistcoat and breeches, and silver lace and buttons. The 1st company had orange-yellow bandoleers and housings; the 2nd had violet bandoleers and housings.

The Gardes du Corps du Comte d'Artois were raised from November 1773, also of two companies, but of 60 men each, and wore a green coat with crimson collar, cuffs and lining, crimson waistcoat and breeches, silver lace and buttons, and crimson housings laced silver. The 1st company had crimson bandoleers and housings; the 2nd had sky-blue bandoleers and housings. The silver lace on the coats, waistcoats, bandoleers and housings was set in a similar way to that of the King's Life Guards. Arms consisted of swords, pistols and carbines. Both units were disbanded in 1792.

Gardes du Corps du Roi de Pologne

(Life Guards of the King of Poland.) The Queen of France was a Polish princess, whose father, King Stanislas, was exiled in 1737. Being also Duke of Lorraine, he took up residence at Luneville. He had a mounted life guard unit forming a squadron of two companies, each of 75 officers and men (including a kettledrummer) which existed from 1737 to 1766. They had two uniforms. The dress uniform was in the Polish king's livery colours: yellow coat with black cuffs, col-

[2] Monsieur was the title given in the French court to the younger brother of either the heir to the throne or the king.

Trooper of the Grenadiers à cheval, c.1721. The most unusual item worn by this unit was the fur-trimmed red cap which pointed towards the back, the only unit in the army to have such a headress. Sketch by Lucien Rousselot after original by Delaistre. (Anne S.K. Brown Military Collection, Brown University)

lar and lining, and silver lace and buttons. The kettledrummer wore the same livery, with the coat almost covered with broad silver lace. The drum banners were yellow, with King Stanislas' coat of arms. The undress uniform was a blue coat with Polish (pointed) cuffs, a scarlet collar, blue waistcoat and silver buttons. The brigadiers had silver buttonhole lace on their coats.

HEAVY CAVALRY

For most of Louis XV's reign the heavy cavalry was officially listed as *cavalerie légère*, 'light' cavalry, a practice that dated back to the 16th century to identify units that were not wearing armour. By the 18th century and influential senior officers such as marshals Villars or Saxe.

A regiment belonged to its mestre de camp, who had bought his command. While a few high noblemen could afford to lavish money on their regiments, the great majority were of modest circumstances, and tried to eke out a profit from their investment in a 'gentlemen's regiment'. Each company in the unit also belonged to its captain, who also had a monetary vested interest in the men they recruited, their arms, clothing, horses and equipment. To make a profit, all had to manage their finances carefully, and this could lead to curious situations: for instance, heavy losses of men, horses and equipment could spell financial disaster. As a result, when on campaign, cavalry pickets would be made up of troopers from many regiments so as to reduce the risk of heavy losses to one unit, a measure that ensured little efficiency and even less cohesion on patrol. Worse, some Mestres de Camp of the 'gentlemen's regiments' were reluctant to commit their units to battle where they might sustain heavy losses!

The proprietary system was finally abolished from 21 December 1762, to the relief of all officers, many of whom were in debt after the disasters of the Seven Years War. From then on the government supplied everything, including horses. The costs were still deducted, but the obligation for captains to make a profit vanished and the sale of commissions, except for the rank of mestre de camp, was forbidden.

Structure

Cavalry regiments had two companies per squadron and usually four squadrons per regiment, although this could vary from one unit to another. Companies generally had as few as 25 troopers per company in peacetime and up to some 50 in wartime. Troopers in the French cavalry were termed *maîtres* (masters). Each company had two to four *carabiniers* (elite men equivalent to infantry grenadiers), a trumpeter, two *brigadiers* (sergeants), a *maréchal des logis* (senior company sergeant), a lieutenant and a captain. If the company carried the squadron's standard, a cornet (or second lieutenant) was included in peacetime. In wartime all companies had cornets.

The regimental staff consisted of the mestre de camp, a lieutenant-colonel, a major, an *aide-major*, an *hautbois* (musician) per squadron and a kettledrummer. An additional lieutenant-colonel, major and aide-major could be added in wartime as well as a surgeon and a chaplain. Thus from 18,300 officers and men in 1740, the line cavalry was able to grow during war to a peak of 38,500 in 1747. This went down to 22,100 until the

Back view of a trooper of the Grenadiers à cheval, c.1721. Sketch by Lucien Rousselot after original by Delaistre. (Anne S.K. Brown Military Collection, Brown University)

armour had long since gone out of use, and 'light' cavalry regiments had actually become the heavy cavalry.

At the head of French cavalry regiments were officials appointed from the high nobility who enjoyed extraordinary privileges but had, by the 18th century, no real power: the Colonel Général, the mestre de camp Général and the Commissaire Général. Each had his own cavalry regiment, which were the first three in precedence. These honorific posts, purchased at high prices, did influence senior cavalry officers' titles: the officer commanding a regiment was termed *mestre de camp* – the equivalent of colonels in other armies. The regimental mestre de camp in fact reported to the men who held the real command power: the minister of war

Seven Years War, and the strength barely increased – only up to 23,200 – in 1760. With peace in 1763 this was reduced again, this time to 14,400, and this rose by barely 2,300 officers and men throughout the rest of Louis XV's reign.

Tactics

French cavalry tactics had not evolved a great deal since the previous reign, in spite of the emergence of light cavalry. Basically, the only real and serious cavalry was the heavy cavalry which charged in close order, boot to boot, and broke the enemy lines. This proved adequate during the wars of Polish and Austrian Succession, but when faced with the superior Prussian cavalry, the French cavalry suffered severe setbacks during the Seven Years War. By 1762, a humiliated country blamed its arrogant cavalrymen, who were now subjected to drastic reductions and reorganisations, measures that eventually forged the peerless cavalry of the Revolution and Empire.

Uniforms

Until 1763 the majority of Louis XV's heavy cavalry regiments wore the grey-white coat that had been introduced in the 17th century. At the beginning of Louis XV's reign and into the 1720s, lapels of the facing colour became fashionable in many regiments. These were very long, reaching from neck to skirt. From 1733 the length of the lapels was ordered reduced, to extend from the neck only to the waist, something that colonels seem to have taken a few years to change. However, some regiments had no lapels.

Another feature in many regiments was the wearing of grey-white cloth buttons rather than metallic buttons. Button placement could vary considerably, but generally there seem to have been three or four per cuff, three to five per pocket and six per lapel. The lining was usually of the facing colour, but could also simply be of the coat colour. A plain strap of the coat colour was on the left shoulder to hold the bandoleer. On the right shoulder was the aiguillette, either flat or of round cord, in the regimental livery colour. Finally, a few regiments experimented with small coat collars.

The waistcoat was, in theory, of buff leather, to protect against sword cuts, and was fastened with brass buttons or, occasionally, hooks and eyes. In practice this warm and often uncomfortable garment was sometimes replaced by a buff cloth waistcoat. The breeches were of a soft buff leather. The boots were of black leather, and reached above the knees. The gloves were buff, the shirt white and the cravat black. The cloak fastened with hooks and eyes at the top, and was long

Drummer of the Grenadiers à cheval, c.1721. The Horse Grenadiers were deemed to be mounted infantry as much as cavalry so they had drummers. They dressed in the royal livery coat of blue lined with red and ornamented by livery and silver lace. The drum was blue with the royal arms painted thereon. Other items were as the men. Sketch by Lucien Rousselot after original by Delaistre. (Anne S.K. Brown Military Collection, Brown University)

and ample. It had a large fall collar and was sometimes lined in the facing colour.

The headwear consisted of a black felt tricorn edged with lace and garnished with a cockade, usually described as black but it has also been shown as white. A steel skull cap would be worn in action. All troopers were also equipped with a steel breast-plate painted black, but this bulky item was unpopular and not often worn, even in wartime. The only regiment that really wore cuirasses, which were made from polished steel with both a breast-plate and a back-plate, was Cuirassiers du Roi.

By the middle of the 18th century the 'fantasy' and frequent changes in dress and equipment were increasingly perceived as being 'contrary to the good of the service'. Reforms were demanded. Following the end of the war of Austrian Succession, in 1748, a board of officers examined the dress, equipment and weapons of the cavalry and recommended a number of changes. These were included in the royal regulation of 1 June 1750.

While the regimental coat and facing colours remained the same, all regiments (except the first three: Colonel-Général, Mestre de Camp Général and Commissaire Général) were henceforth to have pewter buttons (or silver, for officers) and silver hat lace. Lapels on coats were worn by all regiments and, as time went on, nearly all regiments adopted coat linings of the facing colour, turned back. The aiguillette was abolished, and the coat was to have two woollen epaulettes, usually of the colonel's livery colours, with short fringes which were held by two small buttons at each end.

The buff waistcoat was to be of leather, fastened with hooks and eyes, with a small standing collar closing with a small button and with small scarlet cuffs – a fashion already adopted in some regiments.

Breeches continued to be of buff leather when mounted, but were to be of scarlet cloth for duty on foot. The cloak was to be of the coat colour, with a wide turn-down collar. It was to be ornamented at the breast with three wide laces ending in a point, of the same colour as the coat's epaulettes. All regiments were to have tricorns except the foreign corps which had bearskin caps.

Housings for all regiments were henceforth to be blue. Those of royal regiments were to be edged with orange-yellow, which could also have red, white and blue threads mixed in various patterns. Regiments belonging to princes or other nobles and gentlemen would have their blue housings edged with their colonel's livery colours. Only the queen's regiment, La Reine, was allowed its traditional red housings edged with the queen's livery lace.

By and large, the changes specified by the 1750 regulation were adopted, at least initially, but the proud cavalry officers soon felt it was too uniform. From 1756, with war now declared, there came battle reports of men having difficulty in rallying to their regiments or of commanders unable to recognise one unit from another. On campaign and far from Versailles, the officers soon brought in changes in the dress and equipment of their units. Many German units decorated their buttonholes with lace. The use of bearskin caps spread to some non-German units, notably the Cuirassiers du Roi. Aiguillettes continued to be worn in some units, sometimes with an epaulette, and housings changed from blue to red in a few cases.

Troopers were armed with a brass hilted sword, a pair of pistols and a carbine. In each company, two to four elite troopers were armed with rifled carbines (*carabines* – hence their title of *carabiniers*). Officers were armed with swords and pistols only.

Officers wore the same uniform as their men but of better material, with gold or silver buttons, depending on the regimental hat lace. Before 1733 lace on coats and waistcoats could be found, but it was forbidden thereafter. Officers were also supposed to wear cuirasses, but rarely did except for ceremonial occasions or battle.

The Maréchal de Logis (senior company sergeant) had the same dress as the men but of better material, and their housings had a 27mm silver lace. The cuffs of brigadiers (sergeants) had silver edging lace 22mm wide and a wider silver lace of 33mm. The carabiniers had only the 22mm silver edging lace.

Private of the Grenadiers à Cheval of the Guard, c.1750. (Anne S.K. Brown Military Collection, Brown University)

Standard bearer and trooper of the Grenadiers à Cheval of the Guard, 1760. Note the silver grenade which was now added to the cap. The company's one standard was of white silk with gold. (Royal Library, Madrid)

Regiments

The following list describes the main changes which occurred in each cavalry regiment. Their order of precedence in the line varied over the years, especially for the younger regiments. I have used the 1740 and 1758 registers as my main guides. Regimental number is not indicated as they changed frequently and had little importance to French regiments compared with the British army.

Regiments were known by their name, which was often that of a French province, but many were known by the name of their mestre de camp, and these are indicated from 1715 to 1762. Thereafter all the regiments had provincial names, except those belonging to members of the royal and princely families.

The descriptions of the uniforms and housings are given from the earliest fairly complete sources in the 1720s and 1730s, and changes are chronicled up to 1762.

Colonel Général: Members of the Turenne family from 1657 to 1759, 1759 Armand, Marquis de Béthune.

Red coat and lining, black cuffs and lapels, gilt buttons, buff waistcoat with brass buttons, buff breeches, gold-laced hat with black and white cockade, white bandoleer, red cloak. Red housings with standards embroidered and laced with black with a white wavy line in 1735 and black and white checks later.

Mestre de Camp Général: From 1714 Duc de la Vallière, 1716 Comte de Châtillon, 1736 Marquis de Clermont-Tonnerre, 1748 Marquis de Béthune, 1759 Marquis de Castries.

Until about 1736 the regiment had silver-grey coat, red cuffs, lapels and lining, silver buttons and hat lace, white, yellow and grey aiguillette, buff waistcoat, breeches and bandoleer, red housings edged with white, yellow and grey lace with standards embroidered. From c.1736 silver-grey coat and lining, black cuffs and lapels, brass buttons, black and orange-yellow flat aiguillette, buff waistcoat with brass buttons, gold-laced hat with black cockade, yellow bandoleer, silver-grey cloak. Green housings with red standards embroidered and laced orange-yellow, except between 1748 and 1759, when the housings were probably red.

Commissaire Général: From 1714 Comte de Châtillon, 1716 Marquis de Clermont-Tonnerre, 1736 Marquis de Bissy, 1748 Marquis de Castries, 1759 Anne-François d'Harcourt, Marquis de Beuvrons.

Grey-white coat and lining (red until the early 1730s, then black cuffs and lapels), brass buttons, buff

Brigadier of the 1st Company, Musketeers of the Guard, c.1724. Sketch by Lucien Rousselot after original by Delaistre. (Anne S.K. Brown Military Collection, Brown University)

pewter buttons and hat lace after 1750. Blue housings laced white piped red until 1750, afterwards laced with crimson with a white chain.

Royal-Étranger: Blue coat, red cuffs, lapels and lining, pewter buttons, buff waistcoat with brass buttons, buff breeches, silver-laced hat, white bandoleer, blue cloak. Blue coat lining after 1750. Blue housings until 1750; later blue edged, laced orange-yellow with white diamonds, edged blue.

Cuirassiers du Roi: Blue coat, red cuffs and lining, pewter buttons, blue waistcoat, steel breast and back

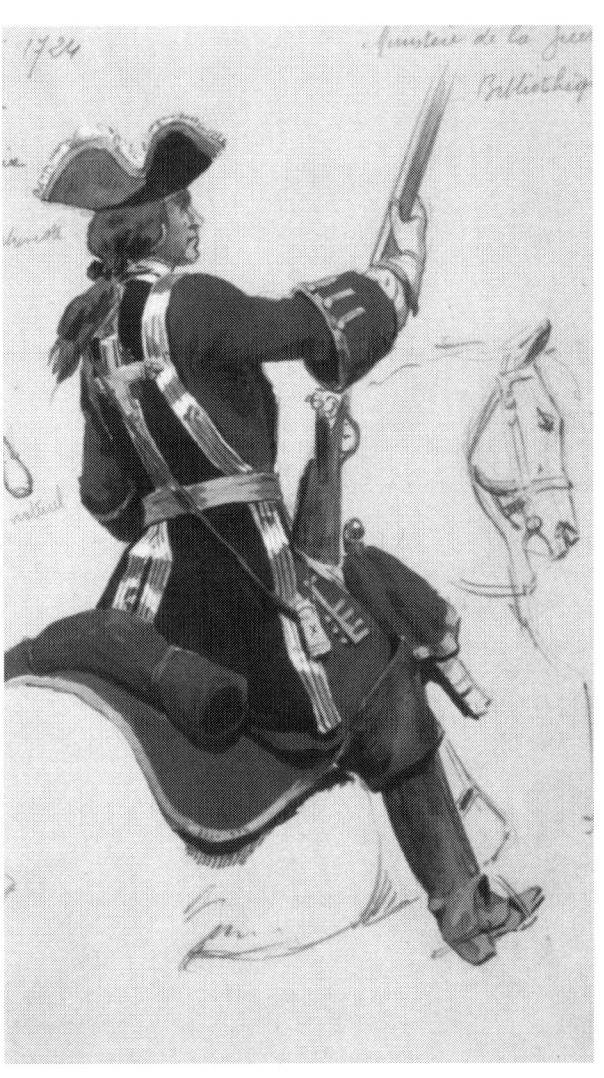

Back view of a Sub-Brigadier of the 1st Company, Musketeers of the Guard, c.1724. Brigadiers had laced buttonholes. Sketch by Lucien Rousselot after original by Delaistre. (Anne S.K. Brown Military Collection, Brown University)

waistcoat with brass buttons, buff breeches, gold-laced hat, white bandoleer, grey-white cloak, red housings until 1750; later red edged laced pale yellow with black zigzags; red and yellow squares from 1759.

Royal: Blue coat, red cuffs and lining, brass buttons (red buttonholes shown in 1735), buff waistcoat with brass buttons, buff breeches, gold-laced hat, white bandoleer, blue cloak. Red coat lapels in the 1740s. Blue coat lining, pewter buttons and silver hat lace after 1750. Blue housings laced yellow with a sun embroidered until 1750; later edged laced orange-yellow.

Du Roi: Blue coat, red cuffs and lining, brass buttons, buff waistcoat with brass buttons, buff breeches, gold-laced hat, white bandoleer and waist-belt, blue cloak; c.1749: buff bandoleer and waist-belt. Blue coat lining, plates with red lining edged white, buff breeches, silver-laced hat, white bandoleer, blue cloak. Black bearskin cap with red lining, white cords and small plume adopted c.1748. Blue housings until 1750; later blue edged, laced orange-yellow with white and red diagonal stripes.

Royal-Cravattes: Blue coat, red cuffs and lining, pewter buttons, white buttonhole lace, buff waistcoat with pewter buttons, buff breeches, silver-laced hat, white bandoleer, blue cloak; from 1750: red lapels, blue lining. Blue housings laced until 1750; later blue edged, laced orange-yellow with blue, white and red squares.

Royal-Roussillon: Blue coat, red cuffs and lining, brass buttons (Gudenus shows pewter buttons and a red aiguillette in 1735), buff waistcoat with brass buttons, buff breeches, silver-laced hat, white bandoleer, blue cloak; c.1749: pewter buttons, waistcoat with hooks and eyes, red aiguillette; from 1750: red lapels, blue lining. Blue housings laced white and red until c.1748, then laced red only c.1749. Later blue housings edged orange-yellow with two blue zigzags.

Royal-Piedmont: Blue coat, red cuffs, lapels and lining, pewter buttons, blue and white flat aiguillette, buff waistcoat with brass buttons, buff breeches, silver-laced hat, wide white bandoleer, blue cloak; from 1750, blue lining. Red housings laced white until 1750; later blue edged laced orange-yellow with small blue, white and red squares.

Royal-Allemand: (German) 'Polish style' uniform: large blue coat, small red cuffs and lining, lace 'brandebourg' and cloth buttons of red, white and blue, red waistcoat edged with white lace and pewter buttons, buff breeches, fur cap with red bag, yellow bandoleer. Blue housings laced white until 1750; later blue edged, laced orange-yellow with red squares.

Royal-Carabiniers: (See Carabiniers, below)

Monteils, 1725 Stanislas-Roi, 1737 Royal-Pologne: Blue coat, red cuffs, small collar and lining, pewter buttons on both sides, blue and white aiguillette, buff waistcoat with brass buttons, buff breeches, silver-laced hat, yellow bandoleer, blue cloak. Red lapels, blue lining from 1750. Blue housings laced white with blue lines until 1750; later blue edged laced orange-yellow with blue and white.

Trooper of the 1st company, Musketeers of the Guard, c.1750. (Anne S.K. Brown Military Collection, Brown University)

La Reine: Red coat, blue cuffs and lining, brass buttons, flat white aiguillette, buff waistcoat with brass buttons, buff breeches, silver-laced hat, wide yellow bandoleer, red cloak. Blue lapels, pewter buttons from 1750. Red housings with a yellow fleur de lis and edged with the queen's livery lace.

Dauphin: Blue coat, red cuffs and lining, brass buttons on each side set in threes, buff waistcoat with brass buttons, buff breeches, silver-laced hat, white bandoleer, blue cloak. Blue coat lining, red lapels, pewter buttons and hat laced silver (after 1750). Blue housings laced orange-yellow until 1750; later blue edged, laced orange-yellow with small blue squares.

Dauphin-Étranger: Blue coat, red cuffs, lapels and lining, pewter buttons, flat white aiguillette, buff waistcoat, buff breeches, silver-laced hat, narrow yellow bandoleer, blue cloak. Blue lining after 1750. Blue housings laced white until 1750; later blue edged, laced orange-yellow with blue, white and red zigzags.

Troopers of the 2nd (left) and 1st (right) companies of the Musketeers of the Guard, 1760. (Royal Library, Madrid)

Bretagne, 1751 Bourgogne: Blue coat, red cuffs and lining, pewter buttons, buff waistcoat, buff breeches, silver-laced hat, white bandoleer, blue cloak. Red lapels, blue lining after 1750. Blue housings laced orange-yellow until 1750; later blue laced orange-yellow with small white squares.

Anjou, 1753 Aquitaine, 1761 Artois: Blue coat, red cuffs, lapels and lining, brass buttons, orange-yellow aiguillette, buff waistcoat, buff breeches, silver-laced hat, wide yellow bandoleer, blue cloak. From 1750: blue lining, pewter buttons. Blue housings laced white in 1735, orange-yellow until 1750; later blue edged laced orange-yellow with blue and red zigzags.

Berry: Blue coat, red cuffs, lapels and lining, pewter buttons, white aiguillette, buff waistcoat, buff breeches, silver-laced hat, narrow white bandoleer, blue cloak. Blue coat lining after 1750. Blue housings laced white and blue until 1750; later blue laced orange-yellow with violet with blue stripes and red and white squares.

Orléans: Grey-white coat, red cuffs, lapels and lining, grey-white buttons on both sides, buff waistcoat with brass buttons, buff breeches, silver-laced hat, narrow yellow bandoleer, grey-white cloak. Red lapels and pewter buttons after 1750. Black bearskin cap from July 1758. Red housings laced white until 1750; later blue laced with a white and blue central stripe, edged with small red and white checks.

Condé: Grey-white coat, red cuffs and lining, grey-white buttons set in pairs, buff waistcoat with brass buttons, buff breeches, silver-laced hat, white bandoleer, grey-white cloak. Red lapels and pewter buttons after 1750. Buff housings laced crimson, with the colonel's arms embroidered until 1750; later blue laced crimson.

Bourbon: Grey-white coat, red cuffs, lapels and lining, brass buttons, red and white flat aiguillette, gold-laced hat in 1735. From c.1736: grey-white coat, red cuffs and lining, grey-white buttons, buff waistcoat with brass buttons, buff breeches, silver-laced hat, white bandoleer, grey-white cloak. Pewter buttons from 1750. Red housings until 1750; later blue edged with crimson and buff lines and white squares.

Chartres, 1724 Clermont-Prince, 1770 La Marche-Prince: Grey-white coat and lining, red cuffs, grey-white buttons, buff waistcoat with brass buttons, buff breeches, silver-laced hat, white bandoleer, grey-white cloak. Red lapels and pewter buttons after 1750. Buff housings laced crimson in 1735; later red housings until 1750, then blue laced crimson.

Villeroy, 1733 Conti: Iron-grey coat, boot cuffs, lining and buttons, orange-yellow aiguillette, buff waistcoat

Officers bearing the standards of the 1st (left) and 2nd (right) companies of the Musketeers of the Guard, 1760. The officers did not wear the blue soubreveste. Each company had six standards for mounted service and an infantry colour when serving on foot. Both standards and colours were of white silk with gold and silver with company badges painted at the centre. (Royal Library, Madrid)

without buttons, buff breeches, gold-laced hat, buff bandoleer, white cloak. Pewter buttons and silver hat lace after 1750. Buff housings with the colonel's arms embroidered until 1750; later blue edged with buff, with red, white and blue central lines.

Toulouse, 1737 Penthièvre: Grey-white coat, red cuffs and lining, grey-white buttons, buff waistcoat with brass buttons, buff breeches, silver-laced hat, white bandoleer, grey-white cloak; c.1749: brass coat buttons, gold-laced hat. Red lapels, pewter buttons and silver-laced hat after 1750. Black bearskin cap from the end of 1758. Red housings edged with livery lace until 1750; later blue edged with blue with a yellow central stripe.

Maine, 1736 Saint-Simon, 1749 Archiac, 1761 incorporated into Du Roi: Grey-white coat and lining, red cuffs and lapels, grey-white buttons, buff waistcoat with brass buttons, buff breeches, silver-laced hat, yellow bandoleer, grey-white cloak. Pewter buttons from 1750. Red housings until 1750; later blue edged with yellow with a green central stripe.

Béringhen, 1718 Conti, 1722 Chayla, 1734 Ancezune, 1740 Du Rumain, 1749 Poly, 1761 incorporated into Royal-Lorraine: Grey-white coat, red cuffs, lapels and lining, grey-white buttons, buff waistcoat with hooks and eyes, buff breeches, silver-laced hat, yellow bandoleer, grey-white cloak. From c.1749: red breeches. Pewter buttons and buff breeches from 1750. Yellow housings until 1750; later blue edged with yellow with a black central stripe.

Du Tronc, 1718 Villars, 1735 Rohan, 1743 Brionne, 1749 Lusignem, 1761 incorporated into Berry: Grey-white coat, red cuffs and lining, pewter buttons, buff waistcoat with brass buttons, red and white aiguillette, buff breeches, silver-laced hat, wide yellow bandoleer, grey-white cloak. Red lapels after 1750. Red then (c.1743) buff housings laced with white and red squares until 1750; later blue laced with blue and yellow squares.

Lambesc, 1730 Beaucaire, 1748 Marcieu, 1761 incorporated into Royal-Pologne: Grey-white coat and collar, red cuffs, lapels and lining, brass buttons, buff waistcoat with brass buttons, buff breeches, gold-laced hat, yellow bandoleer, grey-white cloak; c.1749: pewter buttons set in threes, silver hat lace. Red lapels, and pewter buttons set evenly after 1750. Red housings until c.1748; green edged with livery lace c.1749; later blue edged with blue with a buff central stripe.

Flesché, 1717 Luynes, 1732 Chevreuse, 1736 Ancenis, 1739 Brancas, 1749 Des Salles, 1761 Royal-Lorraine: Grey-white coat, red cuffs and lining, grey-white buttons, red and white aiguillette, buff waistcoat with brass buttons, buff breeches, gold-laced hat, yellow bandoleer, grey-white cloak. Red lapels, pewter buttons and silver hat lace after 1750. Red housings until 1750; later blue edged with black with a red central stripe.

Saint-Aignan, 1717 Russec, 1738 Sabran, 1743 Talleyrand, 1761 incorporated into Royal-Piémont: Grey-white coat and lining, red cuffs, flat pewter buttons, buff waistcoat with brass buttons, buff breeches, silver-laced hat, yellow bandoleer, grey-white cloak. Red lapels and lining after 1750. Red housings until 1750; later blue laced with green and buff squares.

Gesvres, 1740 Clermont-Tonnerre, 1758 Noé, 1761 incorporated into Bourbon: Grey-white coat, red cuffs and lining (Gudenus shows a red collar in 1735), pewter buttons on both sides, red shoulder strap, buff waistcoat edged white with brass buttons, buff breeches, silver-laced hat, yellow bandoleer, grey-white cloak. Red lapels after 1750. Red housings until 1750; later blue edged with blue with a red central stripe.

Latour, 1738 Chabrillant, 1761 incorporated into Royal-Cravattes: Grey-white coat, red cuffs, lapels and lining, grey-white buttons, buff waistcoat with brass buttons, red breeches, silver-laced hat, yellow bandoleer, grey-white cloak lined red. Pewter buttons after 1750. Red housings laced white until 1750; later blue edged with black with a white central stripe.

Heudicourt, 1719 Lorraine, 1734 Lordat, 1738 Rosen, 1744 Egmont, 1756 Charost, 1761 incorporated into Royal-Étranger: Grey-white coat, red cuffs, lapels and lining, pewter buttons, yellow and black flat aiguillette, buff waistcoat with small hooks and eyes, buff breeches, silver-laced hat, narrow yellow bandoleer, grey-white cloak. Yellow housings laced black until 1750; later blue edged with violet with a green central stripe.

D'aubusson Saint-Paul, 1719 Cayeux, 1734 Saint-Aignan, 1742 Beauvilliers, 1761 incorporated into Commissaire-Général: Grey-white coat, red cuffs, lapels and lining, pewter buttons, red and white aiguillette, buff waistcoat with brass buttons, buff breeches, silver-laced hat, yellow bandoleer, grey-white cloak; c.1749: no lapels and grey-white coat buttons; from 1750: red lapels and pewter buttons. Red housings until 1750; later blue edged with red with a buff central stripe.

Tarente, 1719 Turenne, 1735 Grammont, 1759 Balincourt, 1761 incorporated into Royal-Roussillon: Grey-white coat, red cuffs and lining, grey-white buttons, red and green aiguillette, buff waistcoat with brass buttons, buff breeches, silver-laced hat, yellow bandoleer, grey-white cloak. Red lapels and pewter buttons after 1750. Red housings until 1750; later blue edged with green with a buff central stripe.

Vaudray, 1734 Chatelleraut, 1738 Andlau, 1745 Bourbon-Busset, 1761: incorporated into Royal-Picardie Grey-white coat, red cuffs, lapels and lining, pewter buttons, buff waistcoat with brass buttons, buff

Back view of a trooper of the Gendarmerie de France, c.1750. All-red coat with silver buttons and lace, red breeches, red housing laced silver. (Anne S.K. Brown Military Collection, Brown University)

breeches, silver-laced hat, yellow bandoleer, grey-white cloak. Red housings until 1750; later blue edged with yellow with a blue central stripe.

Marsillac, 1716 La Rocheguyon, 1726 La Rochefoucault, 1731 Urfé, 1734 Chatelet, 1738 Fleury, 1743 La Vieuville, 1759 Sainte-Aldégonde, 1761 incorporated into La Reine: Grey-white coat and collar, red cuffs, lapels and lining, grey-white buttons, buff waistcoat with brass buttons, buff breeches, silver-laced hat, yellow bandoleer, grey-white cloak; c.1749: buttons set in pairs, grey undress surtout with Prussian cuffs, red breeches; from 1750: pewter buttons set evenly. Red housings until 1750; later blue edged with blue with a white central stripe.

Saint-Germain-Beaupré, 1717 Brion, 1721 Sassenage, 1740 Maugiron, 1758 Trasségnies, 1761 incorporated into Chartres: In 1735 grey-white coat, red cuffs, and lining, brass buttons, blue, red and white flat aiguillette, buff waistcoat with brass buttons, gold-laced hat, buff bandoleer; from c.1736: pewter buttons, buff breeches, silver-laced hat, yellow bandoleer, grey-white cloak. Red lapels after 1750. Red housings until 1750; later blue laced with violet with buff squares.

Montrevel, 1734 Vogué, 1744 Saint-Jal, 1759 Vogué, 1761 incorporated into Royal: Grey-white coat, red cuffs and lining, pewter buttons, buff waistcoat with brass buttons, buff breeches, silver-laced hat, yellow bandoleer, grey-white cloak. Red lapels after 1750. Red housings until 1750; later blue edged with green with a red central stripe.

Esclainvilliers, 1724 Peyre, 1739 Du Luc, Comte de Vintimille, 1749 Fumel, 1761 Royal-Picardie: Grey-white coat, red cuffs, lapels and lining, grey-white buttons, red, green, black and white flat aiguillette, buff waistcoat with brass buttons, buff breeches, silver-laced hat, yellow bandoleer, grey-white cloak. Pewter buttons after 1750. Red housings until 1750; later blue edged with yellow with a red central stripe.

Villequier, 1723 La Motte-Houdancourt, 1734 Brissac, 1743 La Rochefoucault, 1761 Royal-Champagne: Grey-white coat, red cuffs, small lapels and lining, white collar with smaller red collar on it, pewter buttons, buff waistcoat edged black with brass buttons, buff breeches, silver-laced hat, yellow bandoleer, grey-white cloak. Red housings until c.1748; yellow edged black c.1749; later blue edged with black with a buff central stripe.

Trooper, Colonel Général Cavalry Regiment, 1735, by Gudenus. Red coat and lining, black cuffs and lapels, gilt buttons, buff waistcoat with brass buttons, buff breeches, gold laced hat with black and white cockade, white bandoleer. Red housings with standards embroidered and laced with black with a white wavy line. The regiment was at Philisbourg in 1734 and fought at Klausen in 1735. It was with the army that captured Prague in 1741, at Fontenoy in 1745, Lawfeld in 1747. (Private collection. Photo courtesy U.A. Koch)

Saint-Pouanges, 1716 Chambonas, 1721 Bongars, 1728 Aumont, 1743 Prince-Camille, 1749 Vienne or Damas, 1761 Royal-Navarre: Grey-white coat, red cuffs, lapels and lining, grey-white buttons, buff waistcoat with brass buttons, buff breeches, silver-laced hat, yellow bandoleer, grey-white cloak. Pewter buttons after 1750. Red housings until 1750; later blue edged with red with red central stripe.

Livry, 1718 Bezons, 1723 Beringhen, 1730 Vassé, 1741 Broglie or Broglio, 1752 Lameth-Hennecourt;, 1761 incorporated into Cuirassiers Du Roi: Grey-white coat, red cuffs, lapels and lining, brass buttons, buff waistcoat with brass buttons, buff breeches, silver-laced hat, yellow bandoleer, grey-white cloak. Pewter buttons after 1750. Red housings until 1750; later blue edged with violet with buff central stripe.

La Ferronnaye, 1743 Chabo-La Serre, 1747 Crussol, 1761 incorporated into Orléans: Grey-white coat, red cuffs and lining, brass buttons, buff

Trooper, Mestre de Camp Général Cavalry Regiment, 1735, by Gudenus. Silver-grey coat, red cuffs, lapels and lining, silver buttons and hat lace, white, yellow and grey aiguillette, buff waistcoat, breeches and bandoleer, red housings edged with white, yellow and grey lace with standards embroidered. The regiment served in Italy taking part in the capture of Milan in 1733. Later fought in Prague, Dettingen, Fontenoy and Lawfeld. (Private collection. Photo courtesy U.A. Koch)

waistcoat with brass buttons, buff breeches, silver-laced hat, yellow bandoleer, grey-white cloak. Red lapels and pewter buttons after 1750. Red housings until 1750; later blue laced with violet and white squares.

Germinon, 1723 Lorges, 1728 Durfort, 1733 Randan, 1740 Fouquet, Comte de La Bouchefoliere, 1749 Fleury, 1761 incorporated into Condé: Grey-white coat, small collar and lining, red cuffs and lapels, grey-white buttons, buff waistcoat with brass buttons, buff breeches, silver-laced hat, yellow bandoleer, grey-white cloak. Red lining and pewter buttons after 1750. Red housings until 1750; later blue laced with blue and red squares.

Lénoncourt, 1735 Heudicourt, 1748 Lénoncourt, 1758 Toustain-Viray, 1761 incorporated into Royal-Lorraine: Grey-white coat and lining, red cuffs and lapels, pewter buttons set in threes, buff waistcoat with brass buttons, buff breeches, silver-laced hat, buff bandoleer, white cloak lined red. Red lining, buttons set evenly after 1750. Red housings laced green until 1750; later blue laced with red and white squares.

Chepy, 1744 Bellefonds, 1758 Chartres: Grey-white coat, red cuffs, lapels and lining, pewter buttons, buff waistcoat with brass buttons, buff breeches, silver-laced hat, yellow bandoleer, grey-white cloak. Red housings until 1750; later blue edged with yellow laced with a violet central stripe.

Bouzols, 1719 Brissac, 1727 Cossé, 173 Fiennes, 1747 Saint-Dampieres, 1759 Espinchal, 1761 incorporated into Bourgogne: Grey-white coat, red cuffs, lapels and lining, white cloth buttons set in pairs, buff waistcoat with brass buttons, buff breeches, gold-laced hat, yellow bandoleer, grey-white cloak. Pewter buttons set evenly and silver hat lace after 1750. Red housings until 1750; later blue edged with green laced with a white central stripe.

Novions, 1717 Levis, 1744 Rohan, 1749 Henrichemont, 1759 Escoulombre, 1761 Royal-Normandie: Grey-white coat and lining, red cuffs and lapels, brass buttons, buff waistcoat with brass buttons, buff breeches, silver-laced hat, yellow bandoleer, grey-white cloak. Red lapels and pewter buttons after 1750; from December 1761: red lining. Red housings laced until 1750; later blue laced with red and white squares.

Villepreux, 1717 Russec, 1735 Barbanson, 1748 Moustiers, 1761 incorporated into Royal-Navarre: In 1735: grey-white coat, red cuffs, lapels and lining, brass buttons, white-red-yellow aiguillette, gold-laced hat, buff waistcoat with brass buttons, buff breeches; c.1736 on: pewter buttons, silver-laced hat, yellow bandoleer, grey-white cloak. Red housings until 1750; later blue laced with violet laced with a white central stripe.

Marteville, 1719 Roye, 1725 Du Luc, 1734 Puysieulx, 1743 Saluces, 1759 Seysfelt, 1761, incorporated into Mestre de Camp Général: Grey-white coat, red cuffs and lining, pewter buttons, buff waistcoat with brass buttons, buff breeches, gold-laced hat, yellow bandoleer, grey-white cloak: c.1749: grey-white small coat collar and lining, silver-laced hat. Red lapels and lining after 1750. Red housings until c.1748; green c.1749, later blue laced with green and violet squares.

Rottembourg (German), 1720 Helmstad, 1729 Rosen, 1749 Wurtemberg, 1761 incorporated into Royal-Allemand: Grey-white coat, red cuffs, wide red lapels from neck to skirt, red lining, grey-white buttons, buff waistcoat with brass buttons, buff breeches, silver-laced hat, narrow yellow bandoleer, grey-white cloak. Pewter buttons after 1750. Black bearskin cap from c.1748. Yellow housings laced black, from 1750 blue laced with green and violet squares.

Noailles: Red coat, cuffs and lining, brass buttons, buff waistcoat with brass buttons, buff breeches, gold-laced hat, yellow bandoleer, red cloak. Red lapels, pewter buttons and silver hat lace after 1750. Red housings, then blue housings with violet and yellow squares from 1750.

Béthune, 1735 Pons, 1745 Harcourt, 1759 Preysac, 1761 incorporated into Royal-Champagne: Red coat, blue cuffs and lining (Gudenus shows blue lapels with buttons set in threes, flat white aiguillette, buff bandoleer in 1735) until c.1756, then red cuffs, lapels and lining, pewter buttons, buff waistcoat with brass buttons, buff breeches, silver-laced hat, yellow bandoleer. Red cloak, green housings, blue housings with blue and yellow squares from 1750.

Trooper, Royal Roussillon Cavalry Regiment, 1735, by Gudenus. Blue coat, red cuffs and lining turned back as long red lapels, pewter buttons and a red aiguillette, buff waistcoat with brass buttons, buff breeches, silver laced hat. Blue housings laced white and red. (Private collection. Photo courtesy U.A. Koch)

Trooper, Royal Cavalry Regiment, 1735, by Gudenus. Blue coat, red cuffs and lining, brass buttons, red buttonholes shown, buff waistcoat with brass buttons, buff breeches, gold laced hat. Blue housings laced yellow with a sun embroidered. The regiment was at the sieges of Kehl and Philisbourg and the battle of Klausen, 1734-35, later at Prague, Dettingen, Fontenoy, Lawfeld and the siege of Maëstrich in 1748. (Private collection. Photo courtesy U.A. Koch)

Nugent (Irish), 1735 Fitz-James, 1762 disbanded: Red coat, red cuffs until c.1735 then blue cuffs, lapels and lining, pewter buttons set in pairs, buff waistcoat with brass buttons, buff breeches, silver-laced hat, yellow bandoleer, red cloak. Bearskin cap after 1750. From December 1761, red lining, lapels and cuffs. Yellow housings laced white (housings also described as red), blue housings in 1750; later red housings with white and green squares.

Vaudémont, 1738 Asfeld, 1744 Escars, 1761 incorporated into Penthièvre: Grey-white coat, red cuffs, lapels and lining, pewter buttons, buff waistcoat with brass buttons, buff breeches, silver-laced hat, yellow bandoleer, grey-white cloak. Red housings until 1750; later blue housings with red and green squares.

Raugrave (Belgian – raised 1743), also titled in 1756 Volontaires Liégois, 1758 Cavalerie Liégeoise;, 1762: disbanded: Blue coat, yellow cuffs, lapels and lining, pewter buttons and white lace buttonholes, yellow epaulettes, yellow waistcoat with white buttonholes, buff breeches, bearskin cap, blue cloak

Trooper, Royal Allemand Cavalry Regiment, 1735, by Gudenus. This regiment was noted for its vaguely 'Eastern' dress with a coat featuring slashed sleeves and laces with tassels, fur cap and long moustaches. (Private collection. Photo courtesy U.A. Koch)

lined yellow with crimson and orange lace. Blue housings laced white; from c.1760: laced crimson and orange.

Nassau-Saarbruck (German – raised 1744), 1758 Nassau-Usingen, 1762 disbanded: Blue coat, buff cuffs, lapels and lining, brass buttons and yellow lace buttonholes (pewter buttons and no lace from c.1757), yellow aiguillette, buff waistcoat with small red cuffs, buff breeches, gold-laced hat (bearskin cap from c.1750), blue cloak. From December 1761: brass buttons. Blue housings laced with red and black squares.

Montcalm, raised 1749, 1761 incorporated into Colonel Général: Grey-white coat, red cuffs, lapels and lining, pewter buttons, buff waistcoat with brass buttons, buff breeches, silver-laced hat, yellow bandoleer, white cloak. Blue housings in 1750; later red housings laced with red and yellow squares.

Bezons, raised 1749, 1758 Vaussieux-Héricy, 1761 incorporated into Artois: Grey-white coat, red cuffs, lapels and lining, pewter buttons, buff waistcoat with brass buttons, buff breeches, silver-laced hat, yellow bandoleer, white cloak lined red. Blue housings in 1750; later red housings laced with black and yellow squares.

Corse (Corsican – raised 1757), disbanded December 1762: Small unit of six companies of 25 men each serving in Corsica. Uniform unknown.

Carabiniers

The corps of carabiniers may have been officially styled a cavalry regiment, but it was actually a cavalry division with five regiment-like 'brigades', each having two squadrons of four companies each. This made it the largest unit of line cavalry. It was raised in 1691 by Louis XIV to be an elite corps and given the title of Royal-Carabiniers. Its men were drafted from the better troopers of other line regiments.

Commissions in the carabiniers could not be purchased, but were granted by the king to deserving and talented officers of modest means. Until 1736 it ranked 18th in precedence, then advanced to 12th until 1758, when it was given to the Comte de Provence, thereby losing its 'royal' prefix and becoming the 'Carabiniers de Monsieur' ranking 22nd.

In principle, carabiniers were to fight on foot when required, which they occasionally did, notably when they dismounted, stormed and captured the gates of Prague in 1741. The carabiniers were renowned for their superior horsemanship. From 1763 other line regiments were required to send a few men to be instructed by the carabiniers and this led to the establishment of the cavalry school at Saumur in 1768.

The war record of the carabiniers was distinguished. They served in every campaign, displaying great bravery in victories such as Fontenoy or in defeats like Minden. One of the more spectacular feats by a carabinier occurred at the battle of Lawfeld, on 1 July 1747, when troopers Haube and Ibère captured the British cavalry's commanding general, Lord John Ligonier.

The carabiniers wore the colours of the royal livery: blue coat and small collar, red cuffs and lining (and red collar edged silver from 1757), pewter buttons, silver lace edging the cuffs, white flat aiguillette (white shoulder straps from 1750), buff waistcoat, buff breeches, silver-laced hat with black cockade, white bandoleer edged silver, blue cloak. Blue housings laced white. They were armed as the line cavalry, but their carbines were rifled, and from about 1734 had bayonets. The trumpeters and kettledrummers wore the king's livery until 1758; then that of Provence.

Gardes du Corps, mid-18th century
1: Trooper, Scottish Company
2: Trooper, First French Company
3: Trooper, Third French Company
4: Kettle drummer, Second French Company

Gendarmes and Chevaux-légers Guard Companies, mid-18th century

1: Trooper, Gendarme Company
2: Trooper, Chevaux-légers Company
3: Gendarmes Company trumpeter
4: Chevaux-légers Company trumpeter

Mousquetaires and Grenadiers à Cheval, mid-18th century
1: Trooper, Mousquetaire, First Company
2: Drummer, Mousquetaire, Second Company
3: Trooper, Grenadiers à Cheval

Gendarmerie de France, mid-18th century
1: Officer   2: Trumpeter
3: Trooper, Chevaux-légers du Dauphin
4: Trooper, Gendarmes du Dauphin
5: Trooper, Chevaux-légers de Bretagne

Cavalry of the line, 1740s and 1750s
1: Trooper, Cuirassiers du Roi Regiment, 1740s
2: Trooper, Wurtemberg Regiment, c.1756-1761
3: Cavalry trooper
4: Kettle-drummer, Condé Cavalry Regiment

Cavalry of the line, 1730s–1750s
1: Officer, Nassau-Saarbruck Cavalry Regiment, c.1752
2: Trooper, Rohan Cavalry Regiment
3 & 4: Cavalry officer and trooper, 1740s and 1750s

Dragoon Regiment, 1720s-1750s
1: Drummer and hautbois, Beaufremont Dragoon Regiment, c.1724
2: Trooper, Nicolai Dragoon Regiment, c.1730
3: Trooper, Du Roi Dragoon Regiment, c.1750-1756

Post-1760 reforms

The disasters of the Seven Years War and the ensuing reforms brought about sweeping changes in the French line cavalry. The disappointing performance of the cavalry during the war had numerous causes, ranging from poor organisation to tactical backwardness. On 1 December 1761, the number of cavalry regiments was reduced from 60 to 33, and their organisation standardised to four squadrons each. A year later the last few foreign regiments were disbanded, while training was improved for the others. The gentlemen's regiments disappeared completely, and only a few belonging to princes remained.

The uniforms were also completely revised and were changed considerably in December 1762. Grey-white disappeared as a uniform colour. All regiments now had a blue coat with collar, cuffs, lapels and turn-backs of various facing colours, tricorns, and a generally much more standard appearance. These features were reinforced in regulations of 1767 and later. However, as skilled and organised as it surely was becoming, the heavy cavalry was not to be deployed in war again until the French Revolution.

Trooper, Dauphin Étranger Cavalry Regiment, 1735, by Gudenus. Blue coat, red cuffs, lapels and lining, pewter buttons, flat white aiguillette, buff waistcoat, buff breeches, silver laced hat. Blue housings laced white. The regiment fought at Klausen in 1735. (Private collection. Photo courtesy U.A. Koch)

DRAGOONS

Although a mounted arm, dragoons were considered as horse-carried infantry rather than pure cavalry during the early part of Louis XV's reign. Only half to two thirds of the men had horses. Part of each company served on foot in times of peace, but from 1742 all dragoons were ordered to be mounted. At war's end in 1748, some dragoons were again dismounted as a measure of economy. All were provided with horses at the outbreak of the Seven Years War, a measure that lasted until February 1762, when a third were again dismounted.

The administrative peculiarities with regards to the honorary Colonel Général and mestre de camp Général and the ownership of regiments and companies were the same as outlined above for the heavy cavalry.

Dragoons could be formed into battalions serving on foot during siege operations and ranked as grenadiers heading columns in assaults. They could also act as pioneers to clear enemy obstacles as well as putting up their own abatis. When deployed in the field, they were posted at the flanks of heavy cavalry units, ready to take part in the pursuit following a successful heavy cavalry charge (or an orderly retreat). As time passed, their role gradually became that of medium cavalry, thus filling a tactical vacuum.

Dragoon regiments generally had three squadrons in peacetime, raising up to five during the war of Austrian Succession and four during the Seven Years War. Each squadron had four companies and each company had 25 to 35 troopers in peacetime and up to 40 or 50 in wartime, with a drummer, two brigadiers, one maréchal des logis, one cornet, one lieutenant and the captain. The regimental staff consisted of the mestre de camp, lieutenant colonel, a major, an aide-major and a hautbois per squadron. Dragoon regiments amounted to some 13,600 officers and men during the war of Austrian Succession, and to some 10,700 during the Seven Years War.

Uniforms

Dragoons had colourful uniforms under Louis XIV, a tradition that continued during most of Louis XV's reign, with regiments dressed in red or blue uniforms. Early in the reign the regiments had various facing colours and the coats could have plain or laced buttonholes. The trademark of a French dragoon was his distinctive cap with a bag. Up to about 1733 some units had them trimmed with fur turn-ups, but later on they were made of cloth and the bags became quite long. The men also had a laced tricorn. Another cherished dragoon feature was the aiguillette worn on the coat's right shoulder. Dragoons did not have boots but wore shoes with black leather gaiters that went over the knee and buckled at the side. Stockings were white. Those serving on foot had white infantry gaiters. All troopers were to have a cloak of the coat colour.

The uniform regulation of 1 November 1733 concerning dragoons essentially confirmed the above features but with some changes. The caps were to be of the coat colour, with the turn-up of the facing colour edged with white lace. All buttons were to be of white metal, buttonholes of white lace when worn, and all hats laced silver with a black cockade; however, a few units had gold or yellow lace and probably did not give this up easily. The leather gaiters were to be fastened with brass buttons.

A major attempt to standardise the dragoon's uniforms and equipment came with the regulation of 1 June 1750. The coats and waistcoats had a small standing collar and the buttonholes were laced white and set at equal distances for all regiments except La Reine and Languedoc, which had them in pairs, and Orléans, in threes. All regiments had three buttons at each cuff and pocket except for La Reine and Languedoc. All had pewter buttons. Aiguillettes were abolished, and replaced by an epaulette with fringes on the left shoulder. Breeches were of buff leather for all units; the black leather gaiters were laced up at the side. The cloak was given three laces on the chest, in the same colours as the epaulettes. Belts were to be of white leather.

These uniforms were too similar: eight regiments had a similar dress. Therefore, on 9 April 1757 some regiments were allowed varied facing colours, not only on the coat cuffs but also on small lapels that were added to the waistcoat. Some were also allowed buttonholes set in pairs or in threes. The epaulette was put on the right shoulder and the left shoulder now had a shoulder strap, almost an inch wide and covered with white lace, to hold the cartridge box belt.

Officers had the same uniform colours as their men but theirs was of finer material and the buttons were silver or gold, as was the lace if the regimental uniform featured buttonhole lace before 1750. Thereafter all regiments had such lace, and all officers were to have silver-laced buttonholes. Non-commissioned officers were also to have uniforms of better quality material, but with white material lace. The maréchals des logis, however, were allowed silver lace an inch wide on their housings.

Dragoons were armed with a brass hilted sabre, a pistol fitted with a belt hook and a musket with bayonet. They also carried various tools such as axes, picks and shovels. The saddlery had only one pistol holster on the left side, the right side being a case for a tool.

Regiments

The list below chronicles the main changes which occurred in each dragoon regiment. Most regiments were known by the names of their colonel and these are preceded by the year of their commission.

Trooper, Clermont-Prince Cavalry Regiment, 1735, by Gudenus. Grey-white coat and lining, red cuffs, grey-white buttons, buff waistcoat with brass buttons, buff breeches, silver laced hat. Buff housings laced crimson. The regiment campaigned in the Rhineland, Philisbourg and Klausen in 1734-35. (Private collection. Photo courtesy U.A. Koch)

Colonel Général, from 1704 Duc de Coigny, 1734 Comte de Coigny, 1754 Duc de Chevreuse, 1771 Marquis de Coigny: Red coat, blue cuffs, lining, waistcoat and breeches, pewter buttons, white buttonhole lace, white aiguillette, silver-laced hat with black cockade (in 1735 Gudenus shows white twist cord rather than lace on coat, white lace edging to the waistcoat and no embroidery on housings); c.1724 the cap was shown as of fur with a red bag laced white; in the 1730s, red cap with blue turn-up laced white, red cloak, and red housings laced with white embroidered with royal cypher; from 1750 white epaulette, blue housings laced white; from 1757 white lace edging the waistcoat.

Mestre de Camp Général, from 1709 Comte de Bellisle, 1736 Duc de Chevreuse, 1754 Chevalier de Coigny, 1771 Duc de Luynes: Red coat, cuffs, lining, waistcoat and breeches, pewter buttons, white buttonhole lace, silver-laced hat with black cockade, all-red cap laced white, red cloak, red housings laced with white and embroidered with guidons. From 1750 all-red cap laced black, black epaulette, red housings laced black; from 1757 white coat cuffs and lining, white waistcoat lapels.

Royal: In 1735 blue coat, red cuffs, lining and waistcoat, buff breeches, pewter buttons set in pairs on the breast and in threes on the cuffs, white buttonhole lace, flat white aiguillette, silver-laced hat, blue housings laced with white. From c.1736 blue coat, red cuffs, lining, waistcoat and breeches, pewter buttons set in threes, white buttonhole lace, silver-laced hat with black cockade, all-red cap laced white, blue cloak, blue housings laced with white. From 1750 blue coat lining, blue housings edged with yellow lace with red and white lines, all-blue cap edged with yellow-red-white lace, yellow-red-white epaulette. From 1757 buttonholes set in pairs, waistcoat edged with white lace.

Le Roi or Du Roi: Raised in January 1744 by drafting a company from each of the 15 other regiments. Blue coat, red cuffs, lining and waistcoat, yellow metal buttons, yellow buttonholes on both sides of the coat and on one side only on the waistcoat, yellow aiguillette, gold-laced hat, blue housings laced yellow with yellow fleurs de lis. Cap probably blue with red turn-up laced yellow, blue cloak. From 1750 pewter buttons, white lace, silver-laced hat, blue housings laced white with red and blue, blue cap with red turn-up laced white-red-blue, white-red-blue epaulette. From 1757 buttonholes set in threes, waistcoat with white lapels.

La Reine: Red coat, blue cuffs, lining, waistcoat and breeches, pewter buttons set in threes, white buttonhole lace on both sides, waistcoat with wide white lace edging, silver-laced hat with black cockade, red cap

Trooper, Randan Cavalry Regiment, 1735, by Gudenus. Grey-white coat, small collar and lining, red cuffs and lapels, grey-white buttons, buff waistcoat with brass buttons, buff breeches, silver laced hat. Red housings. The regiment campaigned in Italy in 1733, in the Rhineland, Philisbourg and Klausen in 1734-35. (Private collection. Photo courtesy U.A. Koch)

with blue upturn laced white, red cloak, red housings laced with white. From 1750 housings and caps edged with the queen's livery lace, blue with a white chain, blue and white epaulette. From 1757 red waistcoat lapels.

Dauphin: Blue coat, cuffs, lining, waistcoat and breeches, pewter buttons set in threes, white buttonhole lace on both sides, silver-laced hat with black cockade, all-white cap laced blue, blue cloak, blue housings laced with white. From 1750 housings and all-blue cap edged white speckled with blue, white epaulette speckled with blue. From 1757 buttonholes set in pairs.

Orléans: Red coat and breeches, blue cuffs, lining and waistcoat, pewter buttons, white buttonhole lace, silver-laced hat with black cockade. In c.1724 the cap was of fur with a red bag laced white. In the 1730s red cap with blue upturn laced white, red cloak, red housings laced with blue. From 1750 housings and cap were edged with Orléans livery lace, epaulette of the

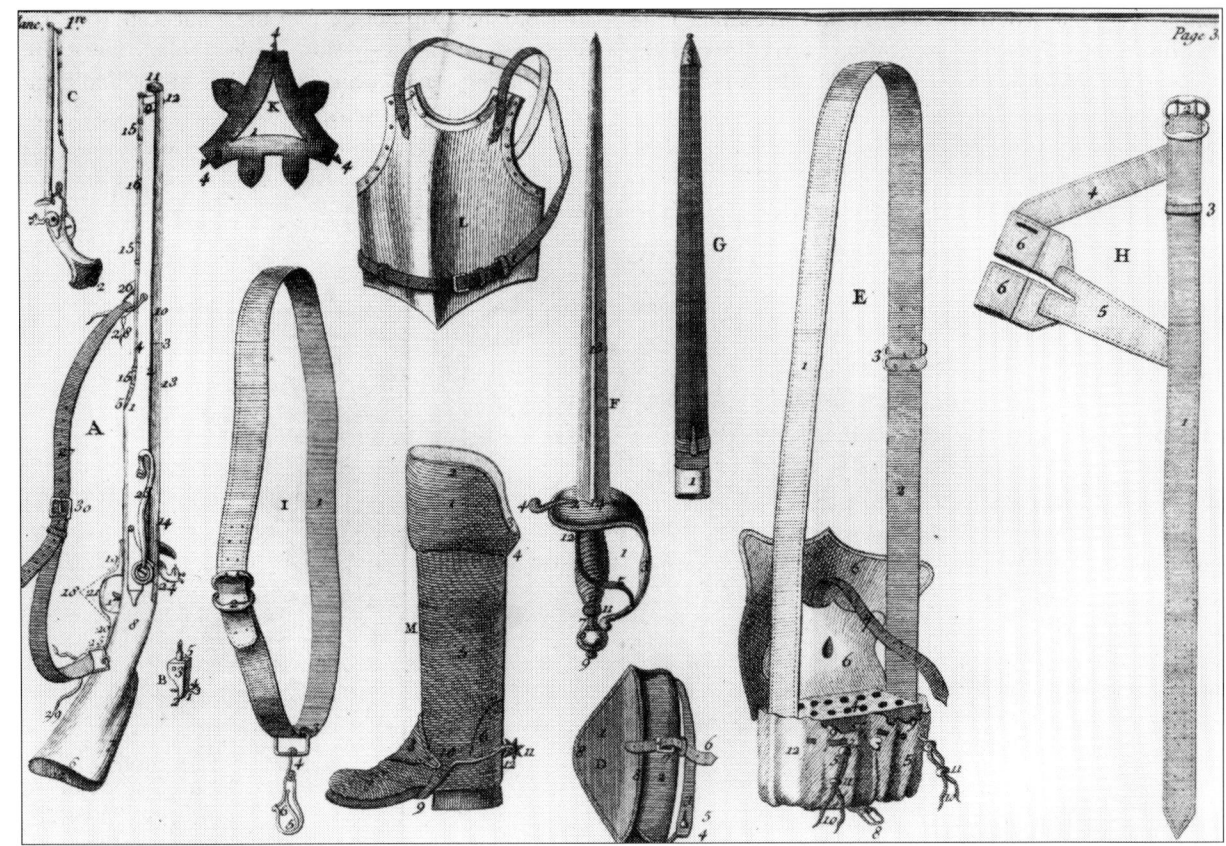

Line cavalry weapons and equipment. At top left, (C) cavalry pistol M.1733, calibre 16.7mm, brass furnishings; (A) cavalry carbine M.1733, calibre 16.7mm, brass furnishings; (K) steel skull cap; (I) carbine belt; (L) breastplate; (M) cavalry boot; (F,G) cavalry sword M.1750 and scabbard; (E) cartridge box with shoulder belt; (H) waist belt with sword frog. (Engraving in La Poterie's Institutions militaires...1754)

same livery. From 1757 buttonholes set in threes.

Beauffremont, 1773 Lorraine: Red coat, cuffs and lining, buff waistcoat, pewter buttons, silver-laced hat with black cockade, buff cap laced with blue plush, buff housings laced with white. From 1750 red housings laced buff, all-red cap laced buff, red and buff epaulette. From 1757 buff coat cuffs, waistcoat lapels and cap turn-up.

Bonnelles, 1727 Amrenonville, 1738 Argence, 1742 Surgeres, 1745 Aubigné, 1761 Choiseul-La-Baume, 1763 Custine: Red coat, cuffs, lining, waistcoat and breeches, pewter buttons, silver-laced hat with black cockade, all-red cap laced white, red cloak. Red housings laced with white. From 1750 red housings laced white with two red zigzags, all-red cap laced white with two red zigzags, white epaulette with two red zigzags. From 1757 light green coat cuffs, waistcoat lapels and cap turn-up.

Espinay, 1734 Vibray, 1745 Caraman, 1761 Antichamp: Red coat and cuffs, blue waistcoat, pewter buttons, white buttonhole lace, silver-laced hat with black cockade, all-red cap with blue upturn laced white, red cloak, blue housings laced with white. From 1750 red waistcoat, red housings laced green, all-red cap laced green, green epaulette. From 1757 green coat cuffs, waistcoat lapels and cap turn-up.

Caylus, 1716 Beaucourt, 1725 Vitry, 1739 L'hopital Saint-Mesme, 1749 La Ferronais, 1762 Rohan-Chabot: Red coat, lining, waistcoat and breeches, blue cuffs and collar, pewter buttons, red buttonhole lace, silver-laced hat with black cockade, orange cap with blue plush upturn laced blue, red cloak, orange housings laced with white and blue. From 1750 red cuffs and waistcoat, red housings laced light blue, all-red cap laced blue, light blue epaulette. From 1757 buttonholes in pairs.

Lautrec, 1720 Rochepierre, 1728 Harcourt, 1758 Flamarens, 1762 Coigny, 1765 Thianges, 1774 Escars: Red coat, green cuffs in 1730; later red cuffs, lining, waistcoat and breeches (Gudenus shows yellow lining and red and yellow aiguillette in 1735), pewter buttons set in pairs, white buttonhole lace, silver-laced hat with black cockade, all-red cap laced white, red cloak, red housings laced with white. From 1750 red housings laced yellow and black, all-red cap laced yellow and black, yellow and black epaulette. From 1757 black coat cuffs, waistcoat lapels and cap turn-up.

Belabre, 1727 Plélo, 1729 Nicolai, 1744 Bertillat, 1748 Apchon, 1761 Nicolai: Red coat and breeches, green cuffs, lining and waistcoat, pewter buttons, white buttonhole lace, silver-laced hat with black cockade, red cap with green turn-up laced white, red cloak, green housings laced white. From 1750 red cuffs, lining and waistcoat, red housings laced blue and orange-yellow, all-red cap laced blue and orange-yellow, blue and orange-yellow epaulette. From 1757 sky blue coat cuffs, waistcoat lapels and cap turn-up.

Saumery, 1731 La Suze, 1744 Asfeld, 1749 Thianges, 1761 Rastignac, 1764 Belzunce: Red coat, cuffs, lining, waistcoat and breeches, pewter buttons, grey buttonhole lace, silver-laced hat with black cockade, all-red cap, red cloak, grey housings laced with livery lace. From 1750 red housings laced white and black, all-red cap laced white and black, white and black epaulette. From 1757 yellow coat cuffs, waistcoat lapels and cap turn-up.

Goesbriant, 1724 Condé, 1740 Mailly, 1744 Egmont, 1753 Marboeuf, 1761 Chabrillant, 1774 Comte de Provence, Monsieur: Red coat, lining, waistcoat and breeches, 'yellowish' cuffs in 1730; in 1735 Gudenus shows crimson cuffs, brass buttons, narrow yellow buttonhole lace, gold-laced hat with black cockade, pale yellow or buff housings laced red. The army register has the same but indicates pewter buttons and white lace, red cap with crimson upturn laced white, red cloak. Red housings laced with white in the 1740s. From 1750 red cuffs, pewter buttons, red housings laced white and violet, all-red cap laced white and violet, white and violet epaulette. From 1757 buttonholes in threes.

Languedoc: Blue coat, red cuffs, lining, waistcoat and breeches, pewter buttons, white buttonhole lace, silver-laced hat with black cockade, blue cap with red turn-up laced white, yellow leather belts, blue cloak, blue housings laced white. From 1750 blue lining and waistcoat, buttons in pairs, red housings laced blue and white, all-red cap laced blue and white, blue and white epaulette. From 1757 red waistcoat lapels.

Septimanie: Raised on 1 March 1744 by the province Languedoc; disbanded in 1749. Red coat and breeches, yellow cuffs, lining and waistcoat, yellow metal buttons, yellow buttonhole lace, yellow-laced hat with white cockade, red housings with yellow lace and yellow cross of Languedoc. The cap was probably red with yellow turn-up.

On 21 December 1762 radical changes were ordered for the corps of dragoons, which were implemented the following year. Unlike the heavy cavalry, the dragoons had distinguished themselves during the Seven Years War. And so, while the cavalry was drastically reduced, the dragoons actually gained a regiment – the

Baron Franz Karl von Reinach-Werth, Nassau-Saarbruck Cavalry Regiment, c.1752. Blue coat, straw buff lapels and cuffs, gold buttons, lace and aiguillette, black breast plate with blue belt and lining edged gold, buff waistcoat laced gold, black bearskin cap with white over blue plume and gold cords. (Private collection. Photo courtesy U.A. Koch)

Baron von Gohr, Rosen Cavalry Regiment, c.1760. White coat, red collar tab, lapels and cuffs, silver buttons and lace, St. Louis cross hanging on a scarlet ribbon, steel breast plate with red lining edged silver, buff waistcoat, black bearskin cap with white tuft and silver cords. (Private collection. Photo courtesy U.A. Koch)

white cloak, housings mostly green with some red and edged with livery lace (usually the same as that adopted in 1750).

Regulations of 1767 and later confirmed the brass helmets and the green coat. It is said that the dragoons became so attached to their brass helmets that they had to be ordered to remove them from their heads when in church. However, dragoons were not to be deployed in war again until the French Revolution.

STANDARDS AND GUIDONS

The basic design went back to an order of 1 February 1684 which required each squadron to have two standards (or guidons for dragoons) in the mestre de camp's livery colour. If not strewn with lilies, the right side was to bear the sun emblem, which during Louis XV's reign included the motto *NEC PLURIBUS IMPAR*. The other side was to have the mestre de camp's *devise* (roughly meaning motto and badge). The *devise* varied considerably according to the mestre de camp's mood. Some simply put on their personal coat of arms and motto, but others would have allegoric scenes painted in a rectangle with a motto that had no connection to the family arms.

The high cost of standards and guidons was often unbearable for the new debt-ridden mestre de camp of a gentlemen's regiment, so many units continued to use the old standards; sometimes out of tradition and attachment as much as for economic reasons. Some units might add new features such as the black border added to Cossé's yellow standards when they became Fiennes Cavalry in 1735.[3] Around 1760 some cavalry regiments started having only one standard per squadron, a measure that had been adopted by dragoons regiments in the 1730s, and made official for all by the orders of December 1762. This rule did not apply to royal guard standards: they had their own rules and unchanging designs, as did the line regiments belonging to princes, and theirs were regularly replaced.

Standards and guidons were made of silk ornamented with gold, silver and silk embroidery and fringes, often mixed together. Although supposed to be of the livery colour, red or crimson silk was favoured

'Volontaires de Schomberg' which became the 17th regiment 'Dragons de Schomberg'.

This unit of dragoons also brought the influence of its radically different uniform to all the dragoon regiments: gone were the tricorns and red or blue coats. The new uniform consisted of a brass crested helmet with a black mane, dark green coat for all with collar, cuffs and lapels in various regimental facing colours, brass or pewter buttons stamped with the regiment's number, aiguillette and fringed epaulette, buff waistcoat and breeches, gaiters replaced by boots, grey-

---

[3] As a result of all these variations it is difficult to identify French line cavalry and dragoon standards and guidons to a regiment. Also, the colour of the standards did not always match the livery colour worn by musicians. The best study to consult for details by regiment is by Pierre Charrié, *Drapeaux et étendards du roi*, Léopard d'Or, Paris 1989.

by many gentlemen's regiments, blue was for royal regiments and white for the royal guard.

Cavalry standards were square and about 50-60cm across. Dragoon guidons ended in the fly in two rounded points and were about 80-100cm high by about 95-125cm in the fly. The pole, including its gilt spear, was about 275cm high, usually painted the same colour as the standard or guidon, though it could also be of varnished natural wood. Just below the spear was tied a white silk 'cravatte' or scarf.

Liveries for musicians

The musicians in the majority of cavalry and dragoon regiments wore the personal livery of their mestre de camp's family. Being, in theory, mounted infantry, dragoons had mounted drummers and hautbois instead of trumpeters and kettledrummers. This was true of cavalry and dragoon regiments belonging to the Colonel Général, the mestre de camp Général and the Commissaire Général. Regiments belonging to the queen also wore her own livery, which was the reverse colours of the king's. Blue coats were strictly reserved for the king's livery, described earlier, worn by the 'royal' regiments as well as by Dauphin, Dauphin-Étranger, Bretagne (later Bourgogne), Aquitaine, Berry and Royal-Carabiniers in the cavalry, Du Roi, Royal, Dauphin and Languedoc for the dragoons. Trumpet and kettledrum banners were usually in the livery colour, with the commander's coat of arms embroidered at the centre and bordered with fringes. Housings tended to be of the coat colour but might also be like the rest of the regiment. White and grey horses were favoured.

The known liveries of mestre de camp of regiments of cavalry and dragoons are as follows:

ANJOU: green lined with orange-yellow; AUBUSSON: yellow, yellow lace with black zigzag at centre and edged with black and white; AUMONT: yellow lined with red, black velvet lace edged with white; BEAUFFREMONT: in 1724 buff lined blue with silver lace, tricorn with blue plumes; BEAUVILLIERS SAINT-AIGNAN: orange-yellow; BÉTHUNE (Armand was mestre de camp Général of cavalry, 1748-59, Colonel Général of cavalry from 1759; Béthune was part of the house of the Duc de Sully): red lined blue, blue worsted lace; BELLEFOND: red; BONNIERES, Comte de SOUASTRE: yellow, blue and yellow lace; BOUFFLERS: green lined red, white lace with red crosses; BOUILLON: white lined black cuffs, the coat garnished with 'brandebourg' lace of black and white silk with tassels; BOURBON: buff lined red, white lace; CASTRIES (the Marquis de Castries was

Trooper, Fitz-James Cavalry Regiment, c.1757-1760. Black bearskin cap with white tassel, red coat, blue collar, cuffs, lapels and turnbacks, white metal buttons, blue waistcoat with red lining edged white, buff breeches, black boots, red housings and buff belts and cartridge box, its flap having an oval brass badge, black sword scabbard trimmed with brass. White and green (or blue) lace edging the lapels, cuffs, buttonholes, housings, belts and cartridge box flap. (Watercolour by C. Becker, Weimar Library)

Commissaire Général of Cavalry, 1748-1759, mestre de camp Général of Cavalry from 1759): green lined red, orange-yellow and black lace; PRINCE-CAMILLE (House of Lorraine): green lined green, plain without lace; CHABRILLANT: red; CHARTRES: red lined blue, blue lace with white and red checked borders; CHAROST: yellow lined blue, velvet lace consisting of red, yellow and blue wavy lines; CHOISEUL: green, silver lace; CLERMONT: light buff lined crimson, crimson slash cuffs, wide silver lace edged with a narrow crimson line on each side; light buff waistcoat edged with livery lace; light buff housings with crimson lace border. Also reported as buff lined red instead of crimson; CRUSSOL: white lined red; CONDÉ: yellow or yellowish buff lined red, red velvet lace; CONTI: pale yellow lined blue, white and blue lace; COSSÉ or COSSÉ-BRISSAC: yellow lined black;

Trooper, Raugrave Cavalry Regiment, c.1757-1760. Black bearskin cap with yellow tassels, blue coat with yellow collar, cuffs, lapels and turnbacks, white metal buttons and white buttonhole lace, yellow waistcoat, buff breeches, white belts and cartridge box with brass badge, black sword scabbard, blue housings edged white with fleurs de lis and crowns, blue cloak and white blanket held by buff belts on the saddle. (Watercolour by C. Becker, Weimar Library)

lace probably blue and buff. The coat had a cross, almost certainly white, on the breast and probably on the back; SAINT-SIMON: yellow; TOULOUSE: red lined blue, yellow lace between two blue laces, slash cuffs and slash pockets; TURENNE (various members of this family were Colonel Général of cavalry from 1657 to 1759): white lined black, black and white checked lace (red housings); VILLARS: brown lined red, crimson and silver lace; VILLEROY: green lined orange, gold and orange lace; WURTEMBERG: yellow lined black, yellow and black lace.

How these liveries were actually worn varied considerably. Generally, the lining colour was applied to the cuffs and lining, and the livery lace used for edging and trimming all seams. Some were fairly plain, while

FITZ-JAMES: yellow; GESVRES: red lined green, wide yellow lace with a green wavy line; GRAMMONT: yellow lined red, blue and red lace; HARCOURT: red lined yellow, red and yellow lace; LORRAINE: green lined green, plain – without lace; LUC: crimson velvet with gold embroidery on all seams; MAINE: red lined blue, yellow lace between two blue laces, boot cuffs and cross pockets; MONTCALM: grey lined red, lace probably yellow and red; NASSAU: orange; NOAILLES: red; ORLÉANS: red lined blue, half white and half blue lace bordered with red and white checks; PENTHIÈVRE: red lined blue, yellow and blue lace; PROVENCE: red lined blue, silver and/or gold lace; LA REINE: red lined blue, blue lace with white chain; ROHAN: red, green and white 'brandebourg' lace; SAINT-GERMAIN-BEAUPRÉ: buff lined blue, waistcoat and breeches, brass buttons,

Officer, Cuirassier du Roi Regiment, c.1750. This portrait of Hubert de Saint-Didier, Baron de Riottier, shows the two main distinctive features in the dress of this regiment. The most evident is the polished cuirass that justified the regiment's name. The second item is the fur cap adopted around 1748, at the end of the War of Austrian Succession, a most unusual item for a French cavalry regiment at that time if frequent enough with foreign units in French pay, probably awarded in recognition of the outstanding services of this unit. The cuirass lining and belts were red edged silver, the coat blue with red cuffs and silver buttons. Baron de Riottier was decorated in 1758 with the cross of Saint-Louis hanging on a scarlet ribbon. It was common practice to add decorations earned later on portraits painted earlier. (Print after portrait)

the coats of others were almost covered with complicated lace patterns. For instance, those of the Colonel Général cavalry regiment in the 1720s feature trumpeters whose white coats were so covered with lace that one could hardly distinguish the basic coat colour. This regiment also had the *NEC PLUS ULTRA* for 18th-century mounted musicians: a black kettledrummer, dressed in livery as the trumpeters except for an exotic white turban with red and yellow ostrich plumes and a gold jewel in front! A fitting tribute from the princely Turenne family to its regiment. Naturally the great majority of kettledrummers in regiments with Mestres de Camp of more ordinary circumstances were Frenchmen, and they wore laced tricorns edged with plumes; turbans were reserved for blacks.

After 21 December 1762 gentlemen's regiments and their liveries vanished and from then on most regiments wore the blue coat of the king's livery with facings of the regimental colour trimmed with the king's livery lace. However, regiments belonging to the queen or princes were allowed coats of their livery colour and the regimental facings trimmed with the regiment's particular livery lace.

All in all, and with such colourful musicians at its head, a French cavalry or dragoon regiment parading in town must have made a magnificent and festive spectacle – and certainly one worthy of the debonair age of Louis XV.

THE PLATES

A: Gardes du Corps, mid-18th century
A1: Scottish Company, trooper
Equipped for duty on foot, he wears red stockings, buckled shoes and a silver-hilted small sword. The carbine hook reveals that the richly laced company bandoleers were nevertheless useful equipment items. Note the powdered hair and black hair bag enclosing the ponytail, fashions prevalent in the senior Guard units and other gentlemen in Louis XV's France.

A2: First French Company, trooper in full battledress
He wears the blackened breast plate, buff breeches and heavy black boots. The edged weapon for battle was a sturdy, straight-bladed cavalry sword with peculiar features for each company which combined luxury with efficiency.

A3: Third French Company, trooper
This trooper is equipped for full dress mounted duty. This was the ordinary dress generally worn by the Gardes du Corps companies for routine patrols or for escorting the carriages of the royal family.

A4: Second French Company, kettledrummer
Musicians of all four companies had similar elaborate silver-laced uniforms but the housings were in the company colour, blue in this case. The kettledrums were covered with superbly embroidered banners with, at the centre, two oval shields, the blue with three gold lilies being the arms of France and the red with gold chains being those of Navarre. This was a tradition observed in many corps that went back a century and a half to the reign of Henry IV who had been King of Navarre before becoming the King of France.

B: Gendarmes and Chevaux-légers Guard Companies, mid-18th century
B1: Gendarmes Company, trooper, full dress
The dress of both companies was generally similar,

Officer, Noailles Cavalry Regiment, c.1767-1770. This portrait shows the considerable changes in the style of the post-1763 heavy cavalry uniform. Nearly all regiments now had blue coats with, for Noailles Cavalry, blue coat cuffs, red collar and lapels, buff waistcoat, silver buttons, lace and epaulettes. (Fortress Louisbourg National Historic Site, Louisbourg, Canada)

Officer, Royal-Allemand Cavalry Regiment, c.1770. The peculiar features worn by this regiment are shown in the portrait of this young officer. Blue coat with red collar, cuffs and lining, silver lace, olivets and epaulettes, buff waistcoat laced silver. (Private collection. Photo courtesy U.A. Koch)

scarlet with black velvet cuffs, except for the lace, which was fully laced in gold for the Gendarmes. The hats were edged with white plumes, the Gendarmes having black cockades.

B2: Chevaux-légers Company, trooper, full dress
This company was distinguished by the silver thread set at the centre of the buttonholes of the coat, narrow silver edging the broad gold lace on the housings and white cockades on the hat. The cloak was rolled up and tied behind the saddle in the first half of the 18th century, the valise being introduced in the latter part of the century.

The French usually disapproved of the questionable practice of docking the tails of horses and achieved the same practical results simply by tying a coloured ribbon around the upper part of the tail, achieving thus a humane and attractive result.

B3: Gendarmes Company, trumpeter
The distinctive red coat superbly laced with gold was allowed for the Guard Gendarme's trumpeters and kettledrummer instead of the blue royal livery. The housings were also red and gold but the trumpet and kettledrum banners were blue with the royal arms and the trumpet had gold cords.

B4: Chevaux-légers Company, trumpeter
The royal livery's blue coat was lined red and lavishly laced with gold and silver. The housings were also blue with gold and silver lace. The trumpet was carried by silver cords slung over the shoulder.

C: Mousquetaires and Grenadiers à cheval, mid-18th century
C1: Mousquetaire, First Company, trooper
The red coats of the Musketeers had little lace, but this was compensated by the superb blue silver-laced soubreveste with crosses on the chest and back, which was their trademark.

Trooper, Colonel Général Dragoon Regiment, 1735, by Gudenus. Red coat, blue cuffs, lining, waistcoat with white edging, blue breeches, pewter buttons, white twist cord buttonholes, white aiguillette, silver laced hat with black cockade. Red housings laced with white. The regiment was at the sieges of Kehl and Philisbourg and the battle of Klausen in 1734-35, fought the Austrians in Bohemia and Alsace in 1742-43. (Private collection. Photo courtesy U.A. Koch)

Consequently, they always wore it, as shown here, with the coat lining turned back for comfort when on campaign. A shoulder-belt would have spoiled the appearance of the crosses so a powder flask on a red and gold cord was carried instead of a cartridge box. The mounted figures in the background show how the musket was carried in the field.

C2: Mousquetaire, Second Company, drummer
The main distinction for the Musketeer's musicians was the heavily laced blue soubreveste, otherwise they generally wore the same red uniform as the men minus the cuff lace. The Musketeers being technically mounted infantry, they had drummers instead of trumpeters and performed both cavalry and infantry drills.

C3: Grenadiers à Cheval, trooper
This trooper is wearing campaign dress. Note the unique shape of the cap's crown worn by these Horse Grenadiers of the Guard. The enlisted men wore moustaches, a distinction of grenadiers in the French army, and they also favoured a long 'rat's tail' style of hair.

D: Gendarmerie de France, mid-18th century
D1: Officer
The coats and waistcoats of the Gendarmerie's officers were richly laced and embroidered with silver at the buttonholes and at the coat seams. Their hats were edged with white plumes.

D2: Trumpeter
Except for the companies of La Reine and Orléans who wore red, the musicians of all other companies had the blue royal livery elaborately laced. Generally, a row of silver lace alternated with a row of the white and red or crimson 'small' royal livery lace with the coat and waistcoat also having white and red or crimson edging lace. The trumpeters' hats were edged with white and red or crimson plumes.

D3: Chevaux-Légers du Dauphin, trooper
The uniform worn by this trooper was similar to that for all companies, be they Gendarmes or Chevaux-légers. It is an all-red coat with a moderate amount of silver lace used only for edging, the troopers' buttonholes having no lace. It was the bandoleers who provided company distinction, the bandoleer shown being light blue edged silver for the Dauphin's Chevaux-légers. The 'light horse' bandoleers were of a lighter hue.

Trooper, Mestre de Camp Général Dragoon Regiment, 1735, by Gudenus. Red coat, cuffs, lining, waistcoat and breeches, pewter buttons, white buttonhole lace, silver laced hat with black cockade. Red housings laced with white and embroidered with guidons. The regiment was at the sieges of Philisbourg and the battles of Ettlingen and Klausen in 1734-35, fought at Prague in 1741, later at Fontenoy and Lawfeld. (Private collection. Photo courtesy U.A. Koch)

D4: Gendarmes du Dauphin, trooper
The same uniform was worn, but the distinctive bandoleer was now a darker hue for Gendarmes. It was nevertheless a practical piece of equipment upon which the carbine was hooked. Housings were red laced silver for all companies except for distinctive company badges or cyphers. In the case of Dauphin, the crowned dolphins (the word 'dauphin' means either crown prince or the sea animal) were the badge of the heir to the throne of France.

D5: Chevaux-légers de Bretagne, trooper
When on manoeuvre or summer campaign, coats were often left aside in favour of the buff waistcoat. For battle, they always charged, and most recklessly, wearing their red and silver uniforms. This company had violet bandoleers.

E: Cavalry of the line, mid-18th century
E1: Cuirassiers du Roi Regiment, trooper, 1740s
This regiment was the only true cuirassier unit in the

Trooper, Royal Dragoon Regiment, 1735, by Gudenus. Blue coat, red cuffs, lining and waistcoat, buff breeches, pewter buttons set in pairs on the breast and in threes on the cuffs, white buttonhole lace, flat white aiguillette, silver laced hat, blue housings laced with white. In 1734, Royal was in Brittany helping tax collectors when it was sent to fight in the Rhineland. (Private collection. Photo courtesy U.A. Koch)

18th-century French cavalry, wearing the front and back plates over the coat fixed with buff and brass belts and buckles. It was considered an elite unit and the men sported moustaches and, from about 1748, bearskin caps.

E2: Wurtemberg Regiment, trooper, c.1756-1761
This trooper is typical of fully equipped heavy cavalry on campaign. The buff bandoleer over the left shoulder was to hook on the carbine's sliding ring, a cartridge box was slung over the right shoulder on a narrow belt, the heavy straight-bladed sword hung from the waistbelt. Note the fringed epaulettes officially in the cavalry worn from 1750. During the Seven Years War, many regiments took to edging their waistcoats with, usually, regimental lace similar to that edging their housings and this is shown here. Bearskin caps were worn by German regiments in French pay.

E3: Cavalry trooper
This back view of a cavalry trooper shows how the accoutrements were worn and hung. The coats were laid aside and only the buff waistcoats worn on manoeuvre and on campaign when it was warm.

E4: Condé Cavalry Regiment, kettledrummer, c.1750
Musicians of regiments owned by princes and gentlemen wore their personal liveries, such as the yellow-buff and red trimmed with silver lace of the powerful and princely Condé family shown here. The kettledrum and trumpet banners of these regiments were in the livery colour of their mestre de camp and were richly embroidered with their coat of arms. In the case of Condé, the banners were yellow-buff with the royal coat of arms thereon, the only difference for Condé being a small red bar between the two upper lilies.

F: Cavalry of the line, 1730s-1750s
F1: Nassau-Saarbruck Cavalry Regiment, officer, c.1752
This figure, based on the portrait of Baron von Reinach-Werth, shows the handsome and elaborate dress of this German regiment in French pay. Officers

Trooper, Condé Dragoon Regiment, 1735, by Gudenus. Red coat, crimson cuffs, brass buttons, narrow yellow buttonhole lace, gold laced hat with black cockade. Pale yellow or buff housings laced red. Sieges of Kehl and Philisbourg, battles of Ettlingen and Klausen in 1734-35. (Private collection. Photo courtesy U.A. Koch)

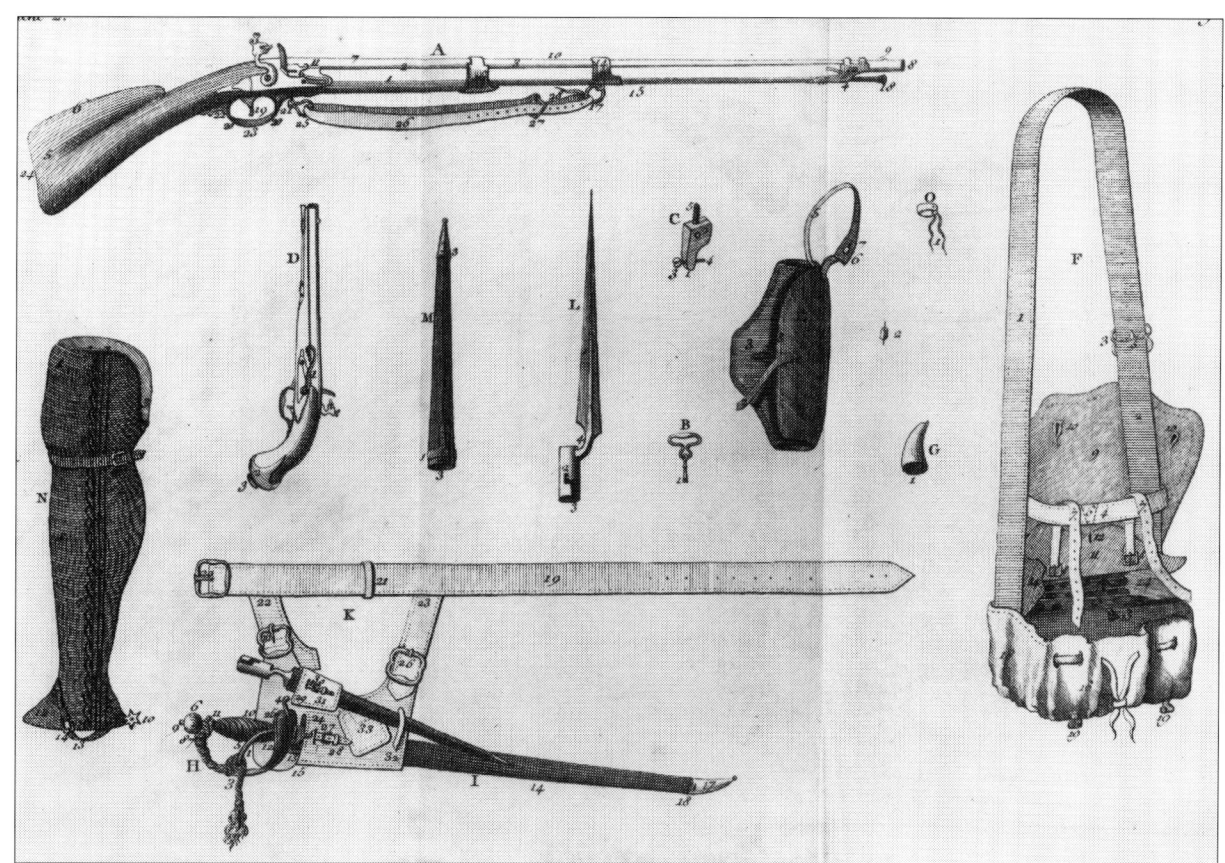

in the line cavalry used flat gold or silver lace aiguillettes on the right shoulder. They were supposed to wear the breastplate, often embellished with gold, but many were loath to wear it even in battle.

F2: Rohan Cavalry Regiment, trooper, c.1735-1743
A common enough morning scene in any cavalry cantonment was this happy trooper carrying his saddle to his horse, wearing the typical dress and equipment of many of the 'grey' line cavalry regiments. The black leather saddle has the pistol holsters in front and the leather socket for the carbine muzzle (see Plate A, figure 3), the grey cloak tied behind and housings appropriate for Rohan.

F3 and F4: La Reine Cavalry, officer and trooper, 1750s
Standard-bearers usually had a bandoleer of the standard's colour edged with gold or silver lace depending on the regiment. This hooked on a sliding ring on the lower part of the standard pike. Officers had the regimental uniform with, in this case, silver buttons and lace on the housings. The troopers of La Reine wore red faced blue, the queen's livery, with housings edged

Dragoon weapons and equipment. At top, the dragoon model musket M.1733, calibre 16.7mm with bayonet and scabbard; below, the cavalry pistol M.1733, calibre 16.7mm which was fitted with a belt hook for dragoons; at left, a dragoon's laced gaiter; at right, the cartridge box with shoulder belt; at the bottom, the waistbelt with sword and bayonet. (Engraving in La Poterie's **Institutions militaires...1754***)*

with the queen's white and blue livery lace. La Reine edged its waistcoats in blue lace rather than livery lace.

G: Dragoon Regiment, 1720s-1750s
G1: Beauffremont Dragoon Regiment, drummer and hautbois, 1720s
Being a 'gentlemen's' regiment, the musicians of this unit wore the buff, blue and silver livery of the Beauffremont family. The dragoons being officially considered mounted infantry, they had drummers rather than trumpeters. The establishment of dragoon (and heavy cavalry) regiments called for a *hautbois* player per squadron and they occasionally were recorded by artists (the one shown here is after Delaistre). It seems some companies had additional hautbois paid by the colonel in some regiments. Another hautbois of Languedoc Dragoons is shown by

above the 30-round cartridge box. The musket is the brass-mounted M.1733 for dragoons. The accoutrement belts were white from 1750, a feature eventually adopted by the whole army. The equipment was similar to the infantry and consisted of a large canvass bag slung over the shoulder. Note the shovel in its leather case on the right side.

H: Dragoon Regiments, 1730s-1762
H1: Languedoc Dragoon Regiment, guidon bearer, c.1735

Dragoon officers wore the regimental uniform in better material using, for instance, silver instead of white lace or aiguillettes. Lacing on the waistcoat was permitted but a plume edging on the hat, apparently especially popular with guidon bearers, might not have pleased inspecting generals. But such plumes could be easily

Black trumpeter of Clermont-Prince's Cavalry Regiment, 1735, by Gudenus. Blacks, in an age when most people in rural Europe had never seen Africans, were especially sought after as musicians in the army, only the most fortunate regiments having them. The wealthy Prince of Clermont made sure his regiment had at least one and had him superbly dressed with a white turban and plume, buff coat with crimson cuffs and lining, silver lace edged crimson, buff housings edged crimson. (Private collection. Photo courtesy U.A. Koch)

Delaistre in the blue and red royal livery but with silver lace possibly indicating that livery lace was reserved for drummers and trumpeters in royal regiments.

G2: Nicolai Dragoon Regiment, trooper, c.1730

The typical appearance of a dragoon in the early part of Louis XV's reign is shown by this trooper. The distinctive dragoon cap was the usual headgear. The musket and accoutrements were generally similar to the infantry's at this time. Dragoons had peculiar saddle holsters: on the right a pistol holster with a green laced white cover; on the left, a tool holster, shown holding an axe encased in black leather.

G3: Du Roi Dragoon Regiment, trooper, c.1750-1756

This dragoon is dressed for service on foot and wearing white infantry gaiters. The tricorn was now the usual headdress and the cap is shown rolled up and tied

Trumpeter, Bourbon Cavalry Regiment, c.1757-1760. Wearing the Mestre de Camp's livery: hat laced silver with buff plumes, buff coat with red collar, cuffs, lapels and turnbacks, white metal buttons and white buttonhole lace, red waistcoat edged with white lace, buff breeches, black boots, white gloves, brass trumpet, brass hilted sword in black scabbard tipped brass, red housings and trumpet banner with white edging, fleurs de lis and crowns. (Watercolour by C. Becker, Weimar Library)

removed before inspection and put on afterwards. The regimental guidon was of yellow silk and gold bearing the arms of the province of Languedoc.

H2: Dauphin Dragoon Regiment, trooper, c.1750-1757

Shown wearing the long cloth cloak with a wide fall collar and regimental laces on the chest according to the 1750 regulations. Cloaks were the same colour as the regimental coat (red or blue), in this case blue, with the regimental white lace with blue ovals.

H3: Apchon Dragoon Regiment, trooper, 1757-1762

From 1757, some regiments were assigned distinctive facing colours to be worn at the cuffs and on small lapels on the waistcoat.

Apchon was assigned sky blue which would have also appeared on the epaulette, hearts on the turnbacks, sword knot and as the turnup on the red cap which is shown rolled above the cartridge box. This trooper also has soft leather boots, which were worn in some dragoon regiments as well as gaiters.

H4: Orléans Dragoon Regiment, trooper, 1757-1762

Orléans always wore red lined blue with, from 1757, the white buttonholes set in threes. This dragoon carries the distinctive accoutrement design for carrying bayonets and swords ordered in 1750.

BIBLIOGRAPHY

Contemporary printed registers of the French army:

Lemau de la Jaisse, P., *Carte générale du militaire de France 1733* and the subsequent annual *Abrégés* up to 1741;

État général des troupes de France, Paris, 1748, 1753;

Dictionnaire militaire, 1750;

Étrennes militaires, Paris, 1757;

État militaire de France, Paris, 1758-1764.

Beneton de Morangue, *Traité des marques nationales*, Paris, 1739

La Poterie, *Institutions militaires à l'intention de la cavalerie et des dragons*, Paris, 1754

Bucquois, L. (ed.), *Fanfares et musiques des troupes à cheval 1640-1940* (plates by various artists), c.1930-40 (repr. 1985)

Mouillard, L., *Les régiments sous Louis XV*, Paris, 1883

Rousselot, L., *L'Armée française, ses uniformes, son armement, ses équipements* (plates published in Paris from 1940s to 1970s)

Susane, L., *Histoire de la cavalerie*, Paris, 1874 (3 vols)

Notes sur les planches en couleur

A: Gardes du corps, milieu du 18ème siècle.
A1 Compagnie Ecossaise, soldat équipé pour l'infanterie, avec des bas rouges et des chaussures à boucle. A2 Première Compagnie Française, soldat en grande tenue de combat, avec la pansière noircie. A3 Troisième Compagnie Française, soldat équipé pour l'infanterie, grande tenue. A4 Seconde Compagnie Française, timbalier. Les musiciens avaient un uniforme similaire mais les caraçaçons adoptaient la couleur de la compagnie.

B: Compagnies de Gendarmes et Chevaux-légers, milieu du 18ème siècle. B1 Compagnie de Gendarmes, soldat en grande tenue. L'uniforme de ces deux compagnies était similaire mais les Gendarmes avaient des galons dorés. B2 Compagnie de Chevaux-légers, soldat en grande tenue. Le fil d'argent au centre des boutonnières et le passepoil en galon doré sur les carapaçons indiquent qu'il s'agit de la Compagnie de Chevaux-légers. B3 Trompette de la Compagnie de Gendarmes qui porte la livrée royale bleue doublée de rouge avec galons dorés et argentés.

C: Mousquetaires et Grenadiers à cheval, milieu du 18ème siècle. C1 Mousquetaire, Première Compagnie, soldat en uniforme de campagne. La doublure du manteau était retournée durant les campagnes. C2 Mousquetaire, tambour de la Seconde Compagnie. En général, ils portaient le même uniforme que les soldats, à part la soubreveste très galonnée. C3 Grenadiers à cheval, soldat en uniforme de campagne. Remarquez la forme très spéciale du calot spécifique à ces grenadiers. Les hommes mobilisés portaient la moustache.

D: Gendarmerie de France, milieu du 18ème siècle.
D1 Officier. Le manteau et le gilet des officiers était richement gansé et brodé d'or. D2 Trompette. A l'exception des compagnies de La Reine et d'Orléans, qui portaient un uniforme rouge, tous les musiciens portaient la livrée royale bleue lourdement galonnée comme illustré. D3 Chevaux-légers du Dauphin, soldat. L'uniforme était similaire pour toutes les compagnies. Les bandoulières faisaient la différence. La bandoulière distinctive était bleu roi bordée d'argent.

Farbtafeln

A: Gardes du Corps, Mitte des 18. Jahrhunderts.
A1 Schottische Kompanie, für nicht berittenen Dienst ausgerüsteter Kavallerist in roten Strümpfen und Spangenschuhen. A2 Erste Französische Kompanie, Kavallerist im kompletten Kampfanzug mit der geschwärzten Brustplatte. A3 Dritte Französische Kompanie, für berittenen Dienst in der Gala-Uniform ausstaffierter Kavallerist. A4 Zweite Französische Kompanie, Paukist. Die Musiker trugen ähnliche Uniformen, doch die Satteldecken waren in der Farbe der Kompanie.

B: Gardekompanien der Gendarmes und Chevaux-légers, Mitte des 18. Jahrhunderts.
B1 Kompanie der Gendarmes, Reiter in Gala-Uniform. Die Uniformen der beiden Kompanien waren im allgemeinen recht ähnlich, nur hatten die Gendarmes goldene Litzen. B2 Kompanie der Chevaux-légers, Reiter in Gala-Uniform. Die Chevaux-légers waren durch den Silberfaden in der Mitte der Knopflöcher und die Einfassung der Satteldecken mit Goldlitzen erkenntlich. B3 Trompeter einer Kompanie der Gendarmes in der charakteristischen, roten Livree der Kompanie mit goldfarbenen Litzen. B4 Trompeter einer Kompanie der Chevaux-légers in der rot gefütterten, blauen königlichen Livree mit Gold- und Silberlitzen.

C: Mousquetaires und Grenadiers à cheval, Mitte des 18. Jahrhunderts.
C1 Mousquetaire, Erste Kompanie, Kavallerist im Feldanzug. Bei Feldzügen wurde das Futter des Waffenrocks zurückgeschlagen. C2 Mousquetaire, Zweite Kompanie, Trommler. Im allgemeinen trugen die Trommler abgesehen von der *soubreveste* mit der üppigen Litzenverzierung die gleiche Uniform wie die Mannschaftsgrade. C3 Grenadiers à cheval, Kavallerist im Feldanzug. Man beachte die einzigartige Form der Mütze dieser berittenen Grenadiere der Garde. Die Soldaten hatten einen Schnurrbart.

D: Gendarmerie de France, Mitte des 18. Jahrhunderts.

Les carapaçons étaient similaires pour toutes les compagnies. **D5 Chevaux-légers de Bretagne**, soldat. Durant les manoeuvres, le manteau était souvent abandonné au profit d'un gilet grège. Les cartouchières de cette compagnie étaient violettes et argent.

E: Cavalerie du front, 1740 à 1759
E1 Cuirassiers du Roi Régiment, soldat, vers 1740. Ce régiment était la seule unité de véritables cuirassiers dans la cavalerie et portait une pansière et une dossière par dessus le manteau. **E2 Régiment de Wurtemberg**, soldat, vers 1756-1761. Durant la Guerre de Sept Ans, de nombreux régiments prirent l'habitude de border leur gilet d'un galon régimental similaire à celui employé sur leurs carapaçons. Les régiments allemands payés par la France portaient des bonnets à poil. **E3** Vue arrière d'un soldat de cavalerie montrant comment les accoutrements étaient portés. Le gilet grège sans manteau était porté durant les manoeuvres et en campagne lorsqu'il faisait très chaud. **E4 Régiment de Cavalerie Condé**, timbalier, vers 1750. Les musiciens de régiments appartenant à des princes et gentilshommes portaient leur livrée personnelle. Ici, il s'agit du jaune, grège et rouge de la famille Condé et leur blason était richement brodé sur les bannières.

F: Cavalerie du front, 1730 à 1759
F1 Régiment de Cavalerie de Nassau-Saarbruck, officier, vers 1752. Ce personnage montre le bel uniforme recherché de ce régiment allemand payé par la France. **F2 Régiment de Cavalerie de Rohan**, vers 1735-1743, qui illustre l'uniforme et l'équipement typique de beaucoup de régiments "gris". **F3 & F4** Officier et soldat de cavalerie, vers 1740 et 1750. Les porte-étendards avaient généralement une cartouchière de la même couleur que l'étendard, bordée de galon doré ou argenté selon le régiment.

G: Régiment de Dragons, 1720 à 1759. **G1 Régiment de Dragons Beaufremont**, tambour et hautbois, vers 1724. Comme tous les "régiments de gentilshommes", les musiciens de cette unité portaient la livrée du Mestre de Camp avec le couvre-chef des dragons. **G2 Régiment de Dragons Nicolai**, soldat, vers 1730, illustrant la sellerie bien particulière des dragons avec une fonte à pistolet sur la droite et une fonte à outils sur la gauche, ici une hache. **G3 Régiment de Dragons du Roi**, soldat, 1750-1756. L'équipement, similaire à celui de l'infanterie, était composé d'un grand sac de toile porté sur l'épaule, Notez la pelle.

H: Régiments de Dragons, 1730-1762.
H1 Régiment de Dragons du Languedoc, porte-guidon, vers 1735. Le guidon du régiment était jaune et portait le blason de la province du Languedoc. **H2 Régiment de Dragons du Dauphin**, soldat, vers 1750-1757, qui porte la cape à galons doubles de ce régiment. La cape était de la même couleur que le manteau du régiment. **H3 Régiment de Dragons d'Apchon**, soldat, 1757-1762. A partir de 1757, certains régiments devaient porter des parements de couleur spécifique sur les manchettes et sur de petits revers du gilet. Il porte également des bottes de cuir souples. **H4 Régiment de Dragons d'Orléans**, soldat, vers 1760, illustrant le type d'accoutrement spécifique conçu pour porter la baïonnette et l'épée.

D1: Offizier. Die Waffenröcke und Westen der Offiziere wiesen eine üppige Litzenverzierung und Goldstickerei auf. **D2** Trompeter. Abgesehen von den Kompanien von La Reine und Orléans, die rot trugen, hatten alle Musiker die blaue königliche Livree, die - wie abgebildet - kunstvoll mit Litzen versehen war. Die Uniform unterschied sich von Kompanie zu Kompanie recht wenig, und lediglich die Schultergürtel waren verschieden. **D4 Gendarmes du Dauphin**, Kavallerist. Das charakteristische Bandolier war silberfarben eingefaßtes Königsblau. Die Satteldecken waren für alle Kompanien ähnlich. **D5 Chevaux-légers de Bretagne**, Kavallerist. Im Manöver entledigte man sich häufig der Waffenröcke und trug stattdessen die gelbbraunen Westen. Diese Kompanie hatte violett- und silberfarbene Bandoliers.

E: Kavallerie der Front, in den 40er und 50er Jahren des 18. Jahrhunderts.
E1 Cuirassiers du Roi-Regiment, Kavallerist, in den 40er Jahren des 18. Jahrhunderts. Bei diesem Regiment handelte es sich um die einzige wirkliche Kürassier-Einheit der Kavallerie. Man trug die Brust- und Rückenplatte über dem Waffenrock. **E2 Württemberg-Regiment**, Kavallerist, ca. 1756-1761. Im Siebenjährigen Krieg machte sich bei vielen Regimentern die Praxis breit, die Westen mit Regimentslitzen einzufassen, die der Litzeneinfassung an den Satteldecken glichen. Die deutschen Regimenter, die in französischem Sold standen, trugen Bärenfellmützen. **E3** Rückansicht eines Kavalleristen, die deutlich macht, wie die Ausrüstung getragen wurde. Die gelbbraunen Westen ohne Waffenrock trug man im Manöver und auf Feldzügen, wenn es heiß war. **E4** Condé-Kavallerieregiment, Paukist, ca. 1750. Die Musiker von Regimentern, die Fürsten und Adligen gehörten, trugen ihre eigene Livree - in diesem Fall ist die gelbbraun-rote Livree der Familie Condé abgebildet - und die Banner waren mit den entsprechenden Familienwappen bestickt.

F: Kavallerie der Front, 30er bis 50er Jahre des 18. Jahrhunderts.
F1 Offizier des Kavallerieregiments Nassau-Saarbrücken, ca. 1752. Auf dieser Abbildung läßt sich die schöne, kunstvolle Uniform dieses deutschen Regiments erkennen, das in französischem Sold stand. **F2** Rohan-Kavallerieregiment, Reiter, ca. 1735-1743, in der typischen Uniform und mit der charakteristischen Ausrüstung vieler der "grauen" Regimenter. **F3 & F4** Kavallerieoffizier und Soldat, in den 40er und 50er Jahren des 18. Jahrhunderts. Die Standartenträger hatten für gewöhnlich ein Bandolier in der Standartenfarbe, das je nach Regiment entweder mit Gold- oder Silberlitze eingefaßt war.

G: Dragonerregiment, 20er bis 50er Jahre des 18. Jahrhunderts.
G1 Dragonerregiment Beaufremont, Trommler und Oboenspieler, ca. 1724. Wie es bei allen "gentlemen's regiments" gang und gäbe war, trugen die Musiker dieser Einheit die Livree des Mestre de Camp mit der charakteristischen Dragonermütze. **G2** Dragonerregiment Nicolai, Reiter, ca. 1730, mit dem eigenartigen Dragoner-Sattelzeug mit einer Pistolentasche auf der rechten und einer Halterung für Werkzeug - in diesem Fall auf der linken Seite. **G3** Dragonerregiment Du Roi, Reiter, ca. 1750-1756. Die Ausrüstung, die der der Infanterie verwandt war, bestand aus einem geräumigen Segeltuchbeutel, der über die Schulter getragen wurde. Man beachte die Schaufel.

H: Dragonerregimenter, 1730-1762.
H1 Dragonerregiment Languedoc, Wimpelträger, ca. 1735. Der Regimentswimpel war gelb und zeigte das Wappen der Provinz Languedoc. **H2** Dragonerregiment Dauphin, Reiter, ca. 1750-1757, im Umhang, dessen Tressen bei diesem Regiment paarweise angeordnet waren. Die Umhänge hatten die gleiche Farbe wie der Waffenrock des Regiments. **H3** Dragonerregiment Apchon, Reiter, 1757-1762. Ab 1757 erhielten einige Regimenter charakteristische Blendfarben, die an den Manschetten und einem kleinen Revers an der Weste zum Vorschein kamen. Außerdem trägt diese Figur weiche Lederstiefel. **H4** Dragonerregiment Orléans, Reiter, ca. 1760. Auf dieser Abbildung sieht man die charakteristische Machart der Ausrüstung zum Tragen von Bajonetten und Degen.